I0157218

The CORRIDOR To CONFIDENCE

*A Step-by-Step Guide
to Cultivating **Confidence** in Prayer*

TREVEAL C.W. LYNCH

The Corridor To Confidence
A Step-by-Step Guide to Cultivating Confidence in Prayer

Treveal C.W. Lynch
Treveal Lynch Ministries International
P.O. Box 12
Pasadena, Ca 91102-0012
Email: confidencetlmi@gmail.com
Website: www.tlmionline.com

ISBN: 978-0-6152-1735-2
Printed in the United States of America
© 2008 by Treveal C.W. Lynch

All rights reserved. No part of this publication my be reproduced, stored in a retrieval system, or transmitted in any form by any means, electronic, mechanical, photocopy, recording, or otherwise, without the prior permission of the publisher, except as provided by USA copyright law.

All Scriptures contained within are taken from the HOLY BIBLE, NEW INTERNATIONAL VERSION®. Copyright © 1973, 1978, 1984 International Bible Society. Used by permission of Zondervan. All rights reserved.

The "NIV" and "New International Version" trademarks are registered in the United States Patent and Trademark Office by International Bible Society. Use of either trademark requires the permission of International Bible Society.

All Definitions contained within are taken from the Merriam-Webster Online Dictionary copyright © 2005 by Merriam-Webster, Incorporated

All rights reserved. No part of the work embodied in Merriam-Webster's pages on the World Wide Web and covered by the copyrights hereon may be reproduced or copied in any form or by any means—graphic, electronic, or mechanical, including photocopying, taping, or information storage and retrieval systems—without the written permission of the publisher.

Cover Art image: Istockphoto
Cover Art work and design by: Young Mi Chi for **ChiStudio**
Interior Art design by: Juan E. Morse for **Juan E Morse Photography**

"Contrary to popular belief and practice, the purpose of prayer is not to solicit God for the things we believe we need.
But rather, to invite God's influence in repossessing what already belongs to us."

- Treveal C.W. Lynch

Dedication

In life we must discover something greater than ourselves to inspire the purpose for which we were sent; for a man's cause can never be himself if he desires to change the world.

What I have discovered are six of the most precious lives God has allowed me to know. First to my wife, Andrea, who is grace manifest, you are truly bone of my bone and flesh of my flesh. You are everything I am not and more than you can imagine, the invaluable being, the rose I discovered among the thorns of life, my heart!

And to my four beautiful children: Treveal, Angelyce, Aaron and Tyler, you are my living favor. I know there is nothing I can or will ever do to deserve such obedient and gifted children. I am overwhelmed daily by the privilege afforded to me by our relationship. You four are much more than I am worthy of raising and qualified to train. I am honored by your lives and the testimony of your nature. I cherish every day with you.

And to my mother Shelia Lynn Lynch who I can no longer touch, yet I continue to feel each day of my life. You expressed your acceptance and love for me no matter what I did or said. You displayed a matchless resolve to give and care for others, one I can only hope to ever achieve. Therefore I dedicate this work and all those to come to you. For without you, there would be no me, I love you, eternally.

Foreword

Spiritual books that successfully inspire and motivate men are few and far between. In most cases, men are either grossly misrepresented or casually lumped into the same category with everyone and everything "Christian". However, there is something to be said about the way men receive inspiration, motivation and, most importantly, information. It must be both relevant and practical, while at the same time, challenging and digestible. As the old saying goes, "*The proof of the pudding is in the eating.*"

It is amazing to me that, in his first attempt, Treveal Lynch has discovered an effective formula for communicating spiritual principles to men. Not only has he captured the attention of a difficult audience, he has also tackled a challenging topic, prayer. While there may be thousands of books on prayer, few of them answer effectively the predominant question on the hearts of ordinary people, "How do I pray?" Most people understand that prayer is important. Few will refute the necessity of prayer. Yet so many Believers fail to sustain an adequate prayer life.

Carefully utilizing the Word of God, this author profoundly establishes proven methodology necessary for men to prevail in prayer. This prayer playbook will definitely introduce much needed transformation to scores of people who may be living beneath their spiritual privilege.

As one who has contributed to his spiritual development, I know that Treveal Lynch practices what he preaches. My prayer is that you, the reader, will embrace the timeless principles within the pages of this book and put them into practice. To God be the glory.

Kerwin L Manning
Senior Pastor / Head Coach
Pasadena Church...*The Church with No Limits*!

Acknowledgments

This book is not only my heart on paper, but the combined inspiration of men that have poured into my life. While I know if I attempt to name each person that contributed to this project I would surely miss several names, I will acknowledge a few of my closest comrades.

I would first like to thank my spiritual father, the great Pastor Kerwin L. Manning. Words can not express the extreme respect and honor I have for you. You are the man I look up to and deem worthy to model my life after. Without your prayers and support, I am sure I would not be the man I am today. From the 6 by 9 cells in country prison to the Saturday morning breakfasts at Denny's in Toledo, Ohio, to today, I have felt and experienced nothing but unconditional love and acceptance from you. I am convinced you have believed in me in the past and that you believe in me now. This book is truly not mine alone, for you taught me to pray. You taught me to rise early and seek God. It was you that sowed the seed that produced a place called confidence in me. I will forever be grateful and loyal to you, your vision and your ministry. I thank you. I love you.

I would also like to thank John "Rusty" Proctor. From the first day we met, you accepted me as I was, despite my tattoos and long ponytail. You helped to transform me into something much greater. As a mentor and friend, your loyalty is unmatched, and your concern for me is priceless. This book would not have been possible without you! Thank you. I love you.

There are few men in life that you can look at and say, "There I am." Yet, when you see them you feel them, you understand them, you relate to them in a way that, no matter the time or season, your friendship is as close as it has always been. Whether in person or in spirit, E. Dwayne Cantrell is that man for me. Brother, you have been more than a mentor, more than someone I can look up to; you have been a living encouragement. Both in

6

business and ministry you have spurred me to heights I never believed I could reach. For this I say thank you. I love you!

Some I call brother, fewer I call friend, and even less I call both. Yet I have found both in Charles Stringer. Charles you have always been a real man to me and have allowed me to see that nothing is stronger than the human spirit. Our relationship is special and I value it deeply. I have watched you grow into a mature and responsible leader over the years, and I truly look forward to seeing and sharing in all God will do through and for you. Thank you. I love you.

To Rudy Carrasco, my main man and mentor, I have learned so much from just watching and listening to you over the few years I've known you. You have and continue to be a mighty influence in my life and the lives of my wife and children. You and your wife Kafi, have loved us in a way that we could not earn on merit or good deeds. You have opened you heart and home to my family and have welcomed a relationship I never could have imagined. You have believed in us and given simple yet profound encouragements that have transformed our thinking and belief in ourselves. You are as responsible for this book as I am! Thank you for accepting me and allowing me to know you more deeply. You are a friend indeed. I love you.

To my little brother Hassan R. Lee, I have seen nothing but the purest of love and dedication to God coming from you since day one! You are young, strong and wise; rare are the men like you, truly there are not enough. You have inspired, encouraged and supported my ministry in ways I'm sure you don't even understand, it is for this reason I say thank you! I love you deeply.

To my brother Damon Lee, in this life there are men sent by God to cultivate the solidity of other men, Damon you are such a man! Although life has thrown our relationship many challenges, I can not and will not deny the significant impact you've had on my life! It was you that taught me to be bold and courageous in the Word of God, to pray with extreme power and to dissect the Word of God for truth and understanding. You were there in the beginning to guide and instruct me in the Word and as a man and for that I will forever be grateful, thank you! I love you.

To the "R.E.A.L. Men (*Respectable, Excellent, Accountable, Leaders*)" of Pasadena Church in Pasadena, Calif., it is with great joy and appreciation that I thank you for being my inspiration. I have enjoyed your fellowship and acceptance since the day I stepped onto West Coast soil. You have done nothing but love me and support me from day one. It is with an overwhelming expectation that I look forward to standing shoulder to shoulder with you as we continue to rebuild the walls in Pasadena and Southern California to the glory of God. I love you all.

And last but certainly not least, to my father, Tarvin West, I would not have been given the chance to experience this life without you! To you, I give my biggest and most sincere thanks. Though we have had much time apart, I am witness to the power of God to keep us connected in mind and heart. I speak like you. I write like you. I fight like you. We share so much, and, yet, there is so much more for us to discover in each other. I thank God for you and our continuing journey. May my accomplishments be your accomplishments! Dad, I value you, I thank you, and I love you.

To the Women

If you are a woman and you have picked up this book, I want to welcome you. I want to encourage you to read on. But, first, I must address a question that is likely to come up as you read through this text. "Why is he only addressing men, as if women don't need to know how to pray? I assure you that no thought could be further from my mind. I know that women need to pray and may need the information contained within these pages. Honestly, if I was writing this book for my own personal gain or ambitions, I might be tempted to do the "politically correct" thing and be inclusive. But I am not writing this book for me. I feel that these words are inspired by God, and I am being true to the voice that is within me. Ladies, I would love for you to read this book to gain an understanding of the biblical calling and responsibilities of the men in your life. There might even be some men in your life that you can pass this book on to once you know its content.

So Treveal, Why Men?

First and foremost, I wrote this book for men as an act of obedience to God. Now, I could go all the way back to the Garden of Eden and bring up facts and figures from the past and present about men. I could go on for pages to prove that men need this book. I could create graphs and charts and talk about the plight of men in our society. I could do all of these things, but doing so would be insincere because I don't need to justify my decision. The honest answer as to why I wrote this book specifically for men is simple, because God told me to! And, while this seems simple, it is actually profound.

I received the vision and inspiration for this book as a result of prayer itself! Funny, prayer does those things; it allows you to hear from almighty God and gain understanding about everything you are supposed to do. So, let this be my conviction, my reason, my explanation: God said so! I am responding to what God told me to do in prayer, and that is good enough for me. I pray that it is good enough for you, too. In fact, I hope that it inspires you to share this book with men in your life that you desire to have the same resolve and peace as I do. This should be the intention of every man: to be able to do what he has been assigned to do, because he knows he can. That's the purpose of this book. That's confidence!

Once again, I encourage you to read on and to share this text with any and every man who has become so confused by the worldly definition of "man" that he does not understand what his responsibility to God is.

To the Men

Brothers, I am that man! I am that man who, to this day, is challenged to rise early and head out for prayer. I am that man who hits the alarm and gets a few more minutes of shuteye. I am that man who looks at himself in the mirror and says, "You know you can do better!" Yes, I am that man who loses focus in prayer. I am that man who has all the challenges that you have and has gone through what you have. I'm that man who makes mistakes and feels that I miss the mark sometimes, too.

I repeatedly tell my wife that, if nothing else, I would leave her a legacy of honesty and faithfulness, and this book will reflect that. Who am I to lie and say I have it all together? What kind of man would I be if I told you I successfully rise every morning and pray for hours on end? What kind of fool would I be to tell you, "I have a *special, personal, direct* line to God?" No, I put my pants on one leg at a time, just like you do; yet, the only difference may be is that refuse to allow it to end there!

I am also a man who has found a way to believe God will answer my prayers. I am also a man who has consistently been given answers to my prayers. I have learned to pray correctly and confidently. I refuse to allow the enemy to take hold of my family and friends. Yet, I am also a man who fights the temptation to sleep in and not pray early in the morning, leaving my pastors and church staff vulnerable. I am a man who knows that life is hard and *chooses* to pray even harder. I am a man who will not stand by idly and let the world I see continue to be the way it is. I am a man who requires of my self what God requires of me – I am a man that prays!

I am a man of prayer!

From the Author

I want every man that picks up this book to know that I refuse to look down on you! I refuse to look down at the man who doesn't get around to praying in the morning. I refuse to speak against the man who fills his schedule up so much that he edges out time for God. No! I won't do it. I declare that you are a good man nevertheless. I believe that you *want* to do what is right. I believe that you want to pray; I know you do! You want to have a better relationship with your Heavenly Father; you want more for your life and those around you. You don't hate to pray. You don't think badly of prayer. In fact, you honestly believe that prayer is necessary. I believe that you instinctively understand that prayer needs to be a part of your daily life. The only thing I question is whether or not you've been taught or given the proper *structure* to pray successfully.

Sure, the preacher tells you to pray. You've read it in your Bible. You remember your grandmother and grandfather praying, and how that may be the only reason you're alive today. You've heard all of the testimonies of prayer, yet you still find it difficult to pray. I'm sure you've been asked about the quality of your prayer life over and over again. Well, in my understanding, "life" refers to something that's living. So, this question would imply that your prayers are alive, active and effective. You may feel, instead, that your prayer life is anything but alive. Not to worry, in the steps that follow, you will receive the structure I spoke of in the previous paragraph. You will discover how to revive your prayers and begin a life of complete confidence!

I sincerely pray that you enjoy and implement these steps into your life and that, in a world filled with fear and insecurity, you discover the confidence needed to become and remain, a man of prayer!

-Treveal C.W. Lynch

THE CORRIDOR

What the Reader Can Expect

The Corridor to Confidence was inspired by my goal to have men know how and why they should pray and, as a result, pray with confidence. I desire to remove one more hindrance in the lives of men and to inspire them to seek God on a greater level. I believe this book will teach men to stand before our Father with confidence and to hear from Him. I believe men want to pray more, but, as with any discipline, we need a plan we can follow. I've read and studied material on the subject of prayer for several years and found that, while it was great information, it was sometimes overwhelming.

Although there is much to say and learn about prayer, I wanted to offer something any man, young or old, longtime believer or new believer, could handle with confidence while growing in prayer. This book will provide the straightforward framework of prayer, a foundation you can build on to know you're doing it correctly! I do not believe that this book is a cure all, for its only goal is to simplify, rather than complicate, prayer. In light of this, you can expect an easy-to-read, easy-to-understand prayer plan. I wrote this book in a step-by-step format to afford you the knowledge that you are following a system as you pray, and, as with anything in life, when you follow the plan, you will have greater levels of success.

In the Beginning

The more I meditate on the roads that led to this book, I realize that my inspiration began years ago, even before I learned to pray. The more I learned of God and His word, the more I desired to become confident in Him, yet something was missing. As I looked to mentors and men that I admired, I began to wonder what they were doing that I wasn't, what they had that I lacked. Why did they seem so confident in God and His Word? Then, it hit me—prayer.

I took notice of the time they spent with God. They were men who came early to church, who knew how to cry out to God and stay in His presence. I remember the first time I was invited to Early Morning Prayer (EMP), it was 6 a.m., and people were awake! I saw my pastor and a small group of people from our church gather in front of our sanctuary and sing and pray with confidence that God would change things in their lives. It wasn't long before testimonies began to come in every morning. People spoke of how God changed their situations and blessed them. That was in 2001.

I soon began experiencing good things in my life. I started sensing that EMP was special. From that time on, I have made it a priority to rise early and seek God before my day begins. I would be a liar if I said I was always successful, but I can tell you that I succeed more often than I fail. I have seen my level of confidence skyrocket and my relationship with God improve by leaps and bounds. My understanding of the Bible and God's plan for me has increased tremendously. Today, I stand as a man convinced that God is willing and able to handle any and all situations that we will encounter.

Where Did this Book Start?

After attending EMP for years, and most of the time with very few men, *if any*, I felt as if God placed a weight of concern on me that I couldn't ignore, *nor did I want to*! I wanted to see my brothers praying and if they weren't, I wanted to know why – I wanted to understand the problem. Yet in my zeal I was tempted to judge, but God quickly helped me acknowledge that just because they weren't *there* didn't mean they didn't pray altogether. Still, I had this weight, a God-driven curiosity. When, one morning in 2006, I was praying at our church alone, and, as I rose from my knees, crying out to God for an answer as to why men are hindered in their desire to gather for prayer, I saw it! From the back of our sanctuary, I could see that in front of every chair stood a man praying. We all came to worship the Lord and believe His word. We were *confident* and strong. We were disciplined, and we had direction and focus. From that vision, came the concept of *confidence in prayer* and more specifically men with confidence in prayer! I see men who are disciplined and skilled in prayer; men who lead their church as soldiers would lead an army into battle. But, as with any army, the soldier must first be trained and prepared for battle. The preparation was where the life of this book began.

As I looked closer at my evolution in men's ministries and my personal relationships with men, I began to sense that many of the men did pray but lacked confidence in their prayers. The Bible says that out of the overflow of the heart, the mouth speaks. In other words, what you say really determines and exposes what you believe! There were times when I'd hear a man pray for healing, yet confess in a conversation a few days later that he was sick. It deeply disturbed me.

Thinking back early on in my prayer life I could remember doing the same things myself and hating it. I hated praying and not knowing if it really worked, if I could really count on God to provide. I didn't enjoy and celebrate prayer, and I don't want any man I encounter to experience that.

From these personal struggles, a passion to teach men to pray with confidence developed in me. I want to uplift men in prayer. I know that some of us may have never entered a time of prayer with an understanding of what to do and what to expect. To walk with God and live a full life, you must develop confidence! The Bible says, *"And without faith it is impossible to please God, because anyone who comes to him must believe that he exists and that he rewards those who earnestly seek him."* -Hebrews 11:6

Not only do you need faith to please God, you need it to even approach Him. It is my belief that true confidence is lacking in the Body of Christ, particularly in our men, and action must be taken! The devil has always targeted our men, seeking to strip us of our confidence and leave us questioning our Father. Sadly enough, it would appear that he's been successful, but I aim to arm you with the tools to defeat him!

How to Use this Book

The best use of this book is as a prayer guide and reminder. I created it in a way that makes it easy to commit the material to memory. Each chapter's name begins with the letter E, and the number of chapters is an even dozen, so remember the 12 E's and you'll do great!

At the end of each *Step* you will find a section titled, "Personal Thoughts and Reflections." I encourage you to use this section to make a note of anything you discover or feel important for you to remember as you incorporate the current Step into your prayer life.

Scriptures are listed by the name of the book, followed by the chapter of the book and the specific verse(s). For example, "Matthew 6:33" would mean the book of Matthew, chapter 6, verse 33.

I have also included examples in each chapter of how I pray to help you get started. I suggest that you take a chapter each day for the next twelve days and focus on that step. Master each step separately first; then, begin to piece them together. You will soon be able to pray through each step in a single prayer. Let me caution you that it may seem like many steps. As with anything, though, the more you do it, the more natural it will feel. Soon, you will begin building on the foundation you lay by following the steps that have been outlined.

Finally, enjoy your time with God. The fact that you are reading this shows God that you are concerned about your relationship with Him. Believe me, He's pleased and will reward you greatly!

So, get ready. Let's pray!

The *E*xplanation

So, what is prayer? Isn't this what we all desire to really know? For, if we have no understanding of prayer, how will we ever pray with confidence, or even begin to pray at all, for that matter. I'm sure you would agree that it would be a good idea to know *what* prayer is and *why* we should do it before we start talking about *how* we do it.

So, What Is Prayer?

I've heard many definitions of prayer, but the common thread that runs through each of them is that "prayer is a conversation between God and man," so I would encourage us to begin there. Just understanding that we need to spend time talking *to* and hearing *from* God is a good start. Others say prayer is "saying back to God what God has already said," and, while this has some truth, it is not completely true, for, if all we did was repeat the Bible, how would we make specific demands on the behavior of ourselves and others. For example, my definition of prayer is: "*successful communication and conversation between God and man*". As in every chapter, I will offer you my personal practices as examples for each step.

But prayer can be described in many ways. Prayer is cultivating God's power in our lives. Prayer is going to the Father of all creation and learning what He desires for and from us and making requests based on our discovery. Prayer is spending time with our Father. Prayer is opening our mouths and commanding what God commands. Prayer is seeking the Word of God and saying in an audible voice, "I agree!" Prayer is receiving the peace of God into our heart and becoming inspired to live upright. Prayer is learning our identity and gaining the confidence to live in accordance. Prayer is, perhaps, God's favorite time of day.

Prayer is being comforted when we fear or worry. Prayer is gaining wisdom for our next move or decision in life. Prayer is cultivating the very confidence of life. Prayer is doing what we were created to do: Commune with God. Prayer is entering a time with God.

I believe it is important to mention, although there are many ways to describe prayer, there is one consistent characteristic of prayer and that is reconciliation. Reconciliation means to settle, bring together and reunite. At the core of any prayer, prayed properly, you will find reconciliation. Throughout the Bible, when ever Jesus prayed, his focus was reconciling us to the Father and the things the Father desired for us to have – *those things that belong to us*! Whether it's our relationship to our Father or receiving healing for our disease, prayer is purposed to reconcile (bring together), the things of God and man.

Lastly, the Bible tells us that Jesus, when questioned by His disciples about how to pray, answered *"This, then, is how you should pray: **Our Father** in heaven, hallowed be your name..."* - **Matthew 6:9** It is important to understand that, as we pray, we are praying to our Father. While we are allowed to acknowledge and speak with the Jesus and Holy Spirit during prayer because they are one; we should always take special joy in our privilege to speak *directly* to our Father! We no longer need anyone to pray on our behalf, when a man is born again (believes that Jesus is the son of God and receives forgiveness for his sins) he is granted personal, one on one communication to the Father, by the blood of Jesus, and empowerment of the Holy Spirit. When Jesus came to Earth, died on the cross, rose three days later and returned to the Father in heaven, He made a way that ALL separation between God and man could be removed; thus reconciling us to the freedom of direct and intimate access with the Father because of His blood and the Spirit which was sent to live in us. So, as you and I pray, we must be confident that we are in a conversation with God Himself, the God that created us. Wow, what an honor and privilege, huh?
So, now, that we are getting a sense of what prayer is, why should we pray?

Why Should We Pray?

To answer this question, allow me to be blunt in saying, we should pray, because WE'RE IN NEED, namely, of a relationship with our Father and the freedom that comes with that relationship. The mere fact you're reading this book and are interested in how to pray is an affirmation of your need for help in life. It's plain and simple, no sugarcoated, lollipop explanation necessary. He's God and we're not, He sees, hears and knows all, while apart from Him, we are extremely deficient in our understanding of life. To understand more of why we need help, I would encourage you, if you haven't already, to read the first 3 chapters of Genesis. There you will discover God's original and perfect intent for mankind – *dominion on the earth*. God said to Himself, "*let them rule*". His commands were clear-cut **"*Be fruitful and increase in number; fill the earth and subdue it. Rule over the fish of the sea and the birds of the air and over every living creature that moves on the ground*"** **-Genesis 1:28**. In other words, God was saying "be like me on the earth, exercise power and rule from a place of authority".

You will also discover how man forfeited that dominion through disobedience and why now need God's influence in repossessing what already belongs to us!

I believe we were created to be earth's **administrator**, our brothers' **advocate** and God's **ambassador**; however, because our position has been abused and abandoned by our embrace of sin, we now stand in desperate *need* of His influence in our daily affairs and moral efforts. Without His power, the "power" we think we have remains useless and ineffective. Yet in His love for us He provided a way to reconnect us to Himself and the intent of our being – a channel back to that power, He gave us *prayer*. Quite frankly, prayer is the only way to enlist the power of God into our lives, and to generate the results we were created to!

So whether your brother is hooked on drugs or your sister is a 14-year-old mother to be, prayer is the answer. The Bible says, "*If my people, who are called by my name, will humble* *themselves and pray and seek my face and turn from their wicked ways, then will I **hear** from heaven and will **forgive** their sin and will **heal** their land.*"**-2 Chronicles 7:14**

The forgiveness and healing of our land is connected to our prayers. Is there a situation in your life that needs healing? Do you have a broken relationship that needs mending, loved ones who need the love of God in their lives? Prayer is the answer. Prayer is our "tool" to fix the world. Prayer gets God's attention like nothing else. The Bible says, **"***Now my **eyes will be open** and **my ears attentive** to the prayers offered in this place. I have chosen and consecrated this temple so that my name may be there forever. My eyes and my heart will always be there*."** -2 **Chronicles 7:15**

God stands at attention when we pray correctly. Imagine that, for a moment, the God who created everything and everyone stands and listens for His "cue," so to speak. When we pray, God hears us and says, "Okay, I can get involved in this person's life now and begin to create for them the life I envisioned at their conception. A life of victory, not defeat; power, not weakness; a life of affiliation with Me, not the destructive ways of the world." Remember, God gave man dominion on the earth. The only way He will get involved is if He is invited. The invitation is called prayer.

Lastly, we need prayer because of our need for a *father's* word. Men, I believe you will be able to relate in one way or another to this example. See, I'm a father of four, and there are times when I will come home and overhear my children playing together in their room and, at some point, one of them will attempt to boss the others around. The child will say something like, "Sit down, you guys, sit down!" and I can hear the others saying, "No." Yet, when I've had a long day and I need some peace and quiet, I will call one of them into my room and tell them to tell the others to sit down. Without fail, they return to the room and say, "*Daddy said*, sit down." Instantly, they all listen. The room is quiet, and everyone is sitting.

Now, why is it that they can say the same thing as before, yet get different results? It was a word from me, the father! This is how God desires us to see Him, as He is, the Father (God) of all creation. And, because He is a Father, His Word carries a father's authority. The Bible says that the fear or (*reverence*) of the Lord is the beginning of wisdom. It goes without saying that it was wise for my children to listen to their sibling I sent with the message because it stopped me from having to pay them a personal visit, which could result in them being corrected, if you know what I mean.

In our lives, we need a word that carries that kind of authority! When the devil attacks your home and tries to destroy you - literally, you need a word that carries authority. This is serious, brothers; this really is life or death. We no longer have time to settle for leftovers when we were created for the feast! Second class citizenship can no longer be tolerated for the kings of the earth. But the battle for Christians' lives is not waged with our physical bodies, but with the sword of the spirit, which is the Word of God. God's Word is our weapon, our power and our life. We need to get a hold of *His* Word daily and pray it to regain our lives and claim the prize set before us. This all begins with a father's word.

So, no longer should we look at our lives and say, "I sure wish things would change. I deserve better, don't I, God?" See, those are our words, and they are power-*less*, but the Father's Word says this;

"*I will listen to what God the Lord will say; he promises peace to his people, his saints, but let them not return to folly. **Surely** his salvation is near those who fear him, that his glory may dwell in our land. Love and faithfulness meet together; righteousness and peace kiss each other. Faithfulness springs forth from the earth, and righteousness looks down from heaven. The Lord **will indeed give what is good**, and our land will yield its harvest.*" **-Psalm 85:8-12**

See the difference? These words are power-*filled* - this is what happens in prayer. You intentionally walk out of uncertainty, fear and the anxiety into assurance, peace and confidence!

The Bible says:

"As the heavens are higher than the earth, so are my ways higher than your ways and my thoughts than your thoughts. As the rain and the snow come down from heaven, and do not return to it without watering the earth and making it bud and flourish, so that it yields seed for the sower and bread for the eater, so is my Word that goes out from my mouth: It will not return to me empty, but will **accomplish** *what I desire and* **achieve** *the purpose for which I sent it."* **-Isaiah 55:9-11**

Brothers, that's powerful; that's *confidence*! That's the kind of assurance and insurance we have when we take the time to get God's Word on a situation. Brothers, I know it gets hard, but there's no "six-headed beast" that can withstand the assault of God's Word, but we must choose to lift the sword and swing – we must choose to pray!

I invite you to read on and discover the steps that lead us to the place called confidence.

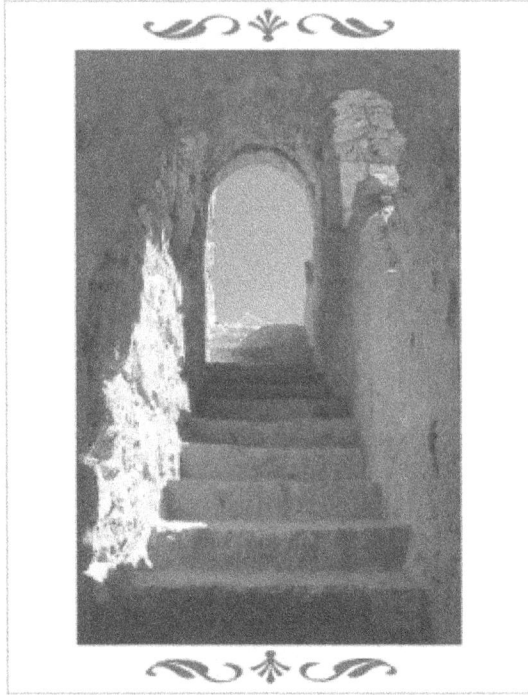

You are now ready to begin taking the steps
toward the place called confidence!

Step I
*E*xpect

"Expectation is the mother of motivation."
- Treveal C.W. Lynch

If you're reading this book, it's likely you either want to learn *how* to pray or learn more about prayer in general. Either way, we will keep first things first. I've learned that, if you start in order, you have a greater chance of finishing in order. Amen!

So, let's start with a question. What do you expect? Wait, what's that you say? You didn't know you needed to expect anything. Well, of course you do. I believe "expectation is the mother of motivation." In other words, I believe expectation gives "birth" to the motivation we need to do anything in life. Think about it. When you and I choose to do something in life, it's likely we've made up our mind as to what will happen as a result of us doing it.

The first and most vital step in a confident prayer life is developing an expectation. An expectation is what you believe you will receive for doing or saying a certain thing. Sure, there are more sophisticated, in-depth definitions, but, as we discussed earlier, that is not the purpose of this book. As we pray, we need to know why we are praying and what we are seeking. In other words, what's our investment in it? I believe that most of us instinctively know that prayer is beneficial. Without an expectation, however, we won't get around to it. An expectation is needed to pray effectively.

Let's ask ourselves what that expectation is—peace, joy, answers to life's tough questions? My job is not to give you all your "why," but, instead, to draw it out from within you. This is so critical that it will make or break your prayer life. You must be honest with yourself. There has to be an expectation, otherwise you will only be going through the motions and end up becoming dissatisfied and disheartened. So, whatever it is, just remember you need to expect it! Whether in prayer or life, if you are not expecting something, it's likely that you won't look for it or do the things necessary to obtain it!

For example, have you ever ordered something in the mail? If you're anything like me, it wasn't long before you started looking for it to come and *expecting* it. The same should be true of prayer. When we pray we should be looking for something. We might seek understanding about a situation in our lives or wisdom to make an important decision or to simply gain a closer relationship with God. We might be praying for something to happen or come into our lives. What it is doesn't matter as much as our expectation of it.

Now, please note, God is not our personal ATM, so don't think just because we expect something, it's ours. There are rules to the game, and the first and main rule is having an expectation. The Bible says, *"And without faith it is impossible to please God, because anyone who comes to him **must believe** that he exists and that he rewards those who earnestly seek him."* -**Hebrews 11:6**

There is nothing worse than praying without expectation. A lack of expectation means that doubt is present. Let's think back to the item you ordered in the mail. You believed that it was on its way, didn't you? Yet, this was something that another man was responsible for providing. Brothers, please don't pray to the God who holds all things in His hand and walk away in doubt. I think you would agree that He deserves more trust than a man we don't even know. The Bible says, *"If any of you lacks wisdom, he should ask God, who gives generously to all without finding fault, and it will be given to him. But when he asks, he must believe and **not doubt**, because he who doubts is like a wave of the sea, blown and tossed by the wind. That man should not think he will receive anything from the Lord; he is a double-minded man, unstable in* *all he does."* **-James 1:5-8** Doubt will cancel your prayers quicker than it took for you to pray.

Before we continue, I'd like to address something that may be an issue for you at first. Are you having trouble coming up with something you believe God can do in your life? Let me suggest one thing I firmly believe we all can expect, no matter our situation or need: inspiration. Merriam-Webster Dictionary defines inspiration as [a divine influence on a person that is believed to qualify the person to receive sacred revelation: the act of drawing in; *specifically*: the drawing of air into the lungs]. We find this definition demonstrated in the book of Genesis, as in the case of Adam. The Bible says, *"The Lord God formed the man from the dust of the ground and **breathed into his nostrils** the breath of life, and the man became a living being."* **-Genesis 2:7** Inspiration is taken from the root word "inspire," which entails an "arousing or start." God literally *inspired* Adam to live! It is the opposite of expire, which entail a "perishing or ending."

When we pray with expectation it allows God to inspire us with new life, understanding and wisdom as we enter His presence. We can expect to be inspired to believe His word concerning us, which produces the confidence we need to obey Him and receive His promises. We can expect to be enthused about our lives and begin to see things differently. Understand that being inspired and enthused leads us to become confident in our prayers. It helps us believe that things will change. Men, we need confidence. We need to know that we have been successful in reaching the Father! This kind of confidence begins to develop when we are inspired, and we are inspired most easily when we enter into a thing with an expectation. Expectation lays a foundation that God can build on. Now that we have our foundation laid, let's begin to build our house of confident prayer!

[Inspiration] definition was used By permission. From *Merriam-Webster's Collegiate® Dictionary, Eleventh Edition* ©2008 by Merriam-Webster, Incorporated (www.Merriam-Webster.com)

How I take this step

"Before prayer, I take a few minutes to quiet myself and think of the goodness of God, past victories and things for which I am thankful. This sets me up to expect more from God. By reminding myself of what He has already done, I can confidently begin to expect even greater rewards. I then do a mental review of my life and reflect on the matters I need to work on, as well as on the needs of those around me. By doing this, I allow God to lead me into a place of expectation. I believe that the inspiration He gives me will help me materialize what I need and desire from Him."

*E*XPECT

PERSONAL THOUGHTS AND REFLECTIONS

_____

_____

_____

_____

_____

_____

_____

_____

_____

_____

_____

_____

_____

_____

_____

_____

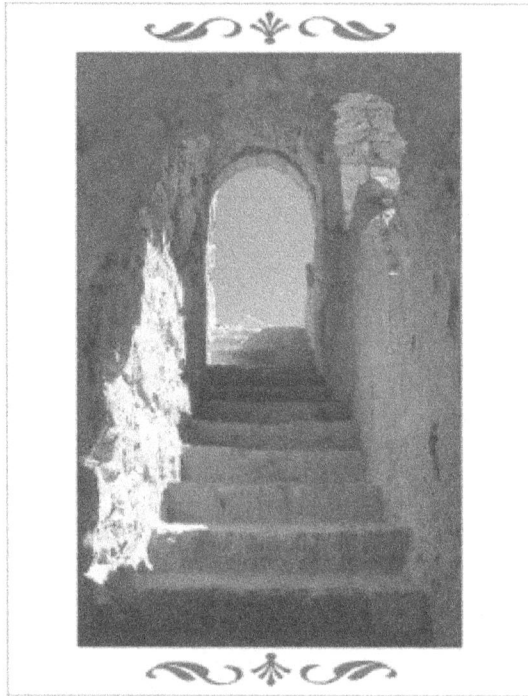

We are now ready to take the next step,
toward the place called Confidence!

Step II
*E*liminate

*"If a man fails to first rule himself,
he will fail to rule anything else."*
- (Author unknown)

Now that we have our foundation laid and secure, we want to begin building on our expectations by taking our second step towards the place we call confidence. The Bible says faith or expectation without tangible evidence is dead, so it is very important to make time and room in our lives to get into God's Word and be able to hear Him when He speaks. In order to do this, we must begin the process of what we call eliminate—the removal of distractions.

Merriam-Webster Dictionary defines distraction as: [mental confusion... to draw or direct (as one's attention) to a different object or in different directions at the same time]—in other words, a lack of focus and control. Men of God, this is no way for us to live, let alone how we should enter into our time of prayer. In fact, the Bible states we have been given what we need to overcome such obstacles. The Bible states *"For God did not give us a spirit of timidity, but a spirit of power, of love and of self-discipline..."* -2nd **Timothy 1:7**

I'd like us to take note of the word self-discipline. Brothers, I won't attempt to sugarcoat this. It's going to require self-discipline to pray and even more so to pray with confidence. Prayer requires a level of focus and a commitment, which is hindered if we are confused or distracted.

[Distraction] definition was used By permission. From *Merriam-Webster's Collegiate® Dictionary, Eleventh Edition* ©2008 by Merriam-Webster, Incorporated (www.Merriam-Webster.com)

On a more practical note, as it relates to prayer, distractions are anything that challenges your attention when you desire to pray. Understand that there will always be things attempting to distract you in life, and they will amplify and exalt themselves most when you decide to pray. In fact, some of them won't become apparent until you attempt to pray. These distractions will come in the form of friends with "urgent" needs, your children fighting over a toy, phones ringing, dogs barking and the list goes on and on. Keep in mind that most of these things are small matters that appear large during our time of prayer. This said, please understand that there are times and situations that require your immediate attention, and you should take proper action when those arise. God gets no glory for us denying the needs of others for the sake of prayer.

You may be wondering if distractions will always pop up, if there are perfect times to pray. The answer is no, but there is a better time, the early morning!

The Bible says, **"*Very early* in the morning, while it was still dark, *Jesus got up*, left the house and went off to a *solitary place*, where he prayed.*"* -Mark 1:35**. This is one of my favorite verses in the Bible, and we will use it as our platform for this step. If you want to do something the right way, who better to learn from than Jesus Himself!

First, the Bible states that it was "*very early in the morning*". I know you may be thinking that the early morning isn't the only time we can pray successfully, and that's a valid point. The fact is, though, distractions become greater as the day goes on. So, while the morning isn't the *only* time to pray, it is a better time to pray.

When I first began to pray regularly, I prayed whenever I got up; no rhyme or reason, just when ever. The problem was the sound of cars going down the street blaring music and the TV in the other room. It was enough to break anyone's concentration.

Then, there was my agenda for the day and all the errands I needed to run.

As soon as I would start praying, my agenda would begin to exalt itself above God. I would begin to think things like, "You don't have time to pray. You need to get ready for work, and, after that, you have to stop by the dry cleaners ..." As I look back, my errands for the day weren't nearly as urgent as they seemed at the time, but, as long as my mind was focused on them, they hindered my ability to pray. The funny thing about distractions is that they don't require you to take action. All they have to do to triumph is get you to invest more thought in them than you invest in God.

The early morning is a great time to pray because when we pray then, we essentially reduce the number of distractions down to ourselves. If you're wondering why I am stressing this, if you're asking if knowing how to pray without distraction is as serious as life or death, the answer is yes. Our lives and those of our families, friends and co-workers are on the line, so we need to pray with clarity and focus. Through our prayers, God could inspire us with ways to improve our marriage or help a sick relative. But, because we choose a few more minutes of shuteye, we miss out.

Brothers, please take no offense. This isn't meant to discourage you but rather encourage you to take prayer more seriously and to remove the distractions that hinder us in prayer. As I've said, morning isn't the only time to pray, it's just the best time to do so, in my opinion. So, if it is possible to pray then, do so. But, keep in mind, the most important thing is that you pray, period!

Another advantage to Early Morning Prayer is that the way we start our day plays a huge part in how the rest of our day goes. Starting our day in prayer is like starting our day with exercise and a healthy breakfast. When we eat properly and exercise, we have more energy and strength throughout our day. The same is true of our spiritual bodies, a good "bowl" of prayer and "workout" of praise and worship fuels us for the rest of the day. This helps to sustain us when we're challenged by the trouble life throws our way.

Secondly, in Mark 1:35, it says that *Jesus got up*! Whether day or night, there is an enemy hell bent on preventing us from reaching our Father. We must decide that what we are expecting to receive in prayer is more important than the distractions we face, including an extra hour of sleep. It's easy to make excuses, to remember the 12-hour workday you had the night before, but you have to push drowsiness and other distractions aside with good old-fashioned determination. Determination is required any time you decide to do something right, let alone pray.

I once heard someone say that prayer is a fight, that it's warfare. In other words, prayer is grown folks' business! Brothers, we must recognize that we are in the fight of our lives. Because we are spirits, the fight is spiritual and the attacks come in spiritual form. Satan is clever and will use distractions that are subtle and appear harmless. Yet, they are filled with poison and aimed to destroy us.

Prayer, while simple in technique, is a very real and grueling fight. It requires us to be men of valor and honor and to have guts and endurance. A man of prayer is nothing short of a hero. Those that choose to partake in the mission of prayer are what I like to call the elite!

Thirdly, Mark 1:35 states that Jesus went to a *solitary place*. Brothers, there is nothing like getting away to a place that you can be in alone, touched by God's presence. I am in no way against group prayer. However, when you find a place that is unoccupied and where you can pray without interruption, amazing things will happen. You will know when you find the right place because you will be free to cry out or yell or dance or lay before God openly. It will be a place in which you can totally be yourself in the presence of the Father. This is vitally important because the feeling of restriction in prayer will prove to be the biggest distraction of all.

I remember when I first began getting away to pray. I didn't want that feeling of restriction. I wanted to feel free to cry out and declare God's Word aloud, so I would go to my car and drive a few blocks down the street. I didn't want anyone to see me yelling and crying in my car and think I was crazy. Funny, huh?

Sometime later I began driving up to the mountains to overlook the canyon and think about how beautiful God's creation was. In the beginning, your getaway place may be your front room at 6 a.m., while everyone else is asleep, or it may be your car, as it was for me when I started. But wherever it is, find it, go there daily and make it your special place. The Bible speaks of God's people naming places because of what God did in that specific place. I believe we should do the same. I have a special row and chair at my church center that I go to when I pray, and God always meets me there. I believe God likes that. When we have that kind of love for Him, He will begin to meet us at our place!

In summary, we can put this step into practice by implementing a plan to remove the distractions that will come up during prayer time. Whether the distractions arise in the early morning or late in the evening, they cause mental confusion and instability. As a result, we never gain the focus necessary to have success in prayer and life. What God desires to share with us is too important to allow our cell phones, barking dogs and daily agendas (which should include time with God anyway) to rob us of a relationship with God and the critical information He has for our lives.

How I take this step

"When I first began eliminating the distractions of life, my concern was silence. I needed someplace quiet, so I simply tried out different places until one spoke to me. I looked for a place that allowed me to speak loudly and be myself. I literally like to cry before God. I like to pray alone. That way I eliminate the temptation to perform, because my prayers can become very intense in nature. My special place is one where I feel free to express myself.

As for daily distractions, I came to a point where I was tired of being "bullied" by life. I felt that, if I kept letting any and everything pull me away from time with God, all I would ever have were distractions, and they were not enough. I want all life has to offer. I want God's best. I know you do, too."

*E*LIMINATE

PERSONAL THOUGHTS AND REFLECTIONS

_____

_____

_____

_____

_____

_____

_____

_____

_____

_____

_____

_____

_____

_____

_____

_____

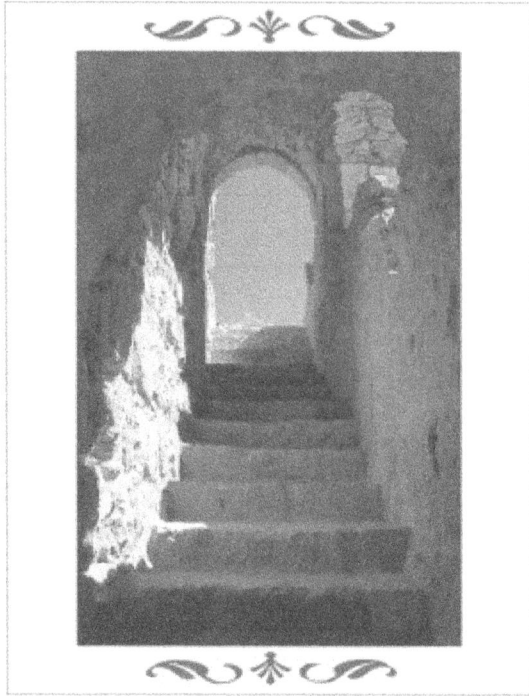

We are now ready to take the next step,
toward the place called Confidence!

Step III
*E*steem

L ook at us, ready for another step! We've done an awesome job. Let's look at what we've accomplished so far. We've gained an expectation for our prayers, and we've removed all the hindrances that attempt to rob us of time with our Father. So, now, we're ready for the third step towards the place we call confidence, esteem! The Bible says, *"Enter his gates with* **thanksgiving** *and his courts with praise; give thanks to him and praise his name."* **-Psalm 100:4**

Notice in this passage there are two instructions for entering God's presence. For now, we'll cover the first. The other we'll cover in Step Four. The first instruction is to enter His gates, or the outer realm (area), with thanksgiving! Before we can get into the inner part of anything we must first pass through the outer! For example, have you ever cooked with fresh garlic? I mean the kind you have to peel yourself. If you have, you know that a clove of garlic has several layers to it. Yet the part of the clove we use to actually cook with is in the center. And so it is with reaching the place of confidence in prayer. The center is where we want to be!

In order to enter the presence of God, where the confidence is cultivated, we enter first with thanksgiving. So, what is thanksgiving, and how do we practice it? Thanksgiving is the time we spend remembering and recalling what God has done and promised to do. This is where we acknowledge the fact that God is responsible for giving us our very lives. It is the time we invest in rejoicing in God's mercy and grace. This is where we say aloud, "Thank you, Father, for rescuing me from a life that was headed for destruction and regret." This is also where we say, "thank you God for keeping me safe from unseen danger that, if not for you, I would have been harmed by." This is personal for all of us. We all have different things for which to give thanks. For you, it may be thanking God for healing you of cancer. For another, it may be thanking God for the ability to buy a home. Whatever it is, thank Him for it! Tell Him that it is because of Him that the sun will rise today. Tell Him that it is because of Him that you're in your right mind. Tell Him that you know that it was not you and your intelligence but He that helped you in your time of need.

You may notice that I will spend more time and text on this step than I do many of the others, and for good reason. This step deals directly with our attitude. It deals with our ability to humble ourselves and confess that we need God's help. If we can't complete this step, the corridor to confidence will quickly grow too narrow for us to travel.

Now, I'd like to address two huge misconceptions about prayer. Firstly, we should understand that when we thank God, we should always thank Him for who he is, not only for what He does. Remember God is a God of integrity. This means He can be totally trusted. Can we think of one person in our lives that we can totally trust, just one? When I say trust I mean the kind of trust that indicates that they can't fail us, not because they don't want to fail us, but because they don't have the ability to fail us. No? Me either!

Let's face it. Everyone makes mistakes, but not God. He can't change because His word and plans flow together in perfect unity. He and His word are one in the same. The Bible says, *"In the beginning was the Word, and the Word was with God, and the Word was God."* **-John 1:1** This means that, if God were to ever lie or do something contrary to His Word, He ceases to be God! So, remember to take time to say, "God, I thank you because you are you. You don't change. You are the God of integrity, and I thank you because I can trust in your character."

The second misconception is that our definition of "good" is the same as God's. See, we tend to think of good as things that make us happy or feel good to us. We tend to put too much value on the feelings of life. Our society is one that trains and promotes self-indulgence and pleasing ourselves. There's even a popular restaurant chain that carries the tagline, *"Have it your way."*

We have adopted a twisted philosophy of what good is and is not. Imagine if God had said, "Have it your way." We would have destroyed ourselves centuries ago! Now, brothers, please understand that I'm not anti-pleasure. Yet, I'm not anti-pain, either.

We need to understand that God's idea of good is things that promote holiness and righteousness. These things may not look or feel good to us, but they are the very things that help us the most. I say this because there are times when God allows painful things to enter our lives. At first glance, they seem to be for our destruction. Yet, when we enter His presence, we're given new eyes that have the ability to see those same things in full perspective, and it is revealed that they are actually created for our good!

For example, I recently had a situation in my work life that challenged my very character. I had been working for a company in a location and with a team I loved for over a year when I was sent to another location to work in that was very uncomfortable. When I first arrived, I sensed that I would be miserable. I was bent on finding all the "bad" things I could find to justify my cloudy perspective. As I began working there, I discovered that things were not being run the way I believed they should have been. Because I was new to the area, I felt I had no power to change anything or anyone, which made it worse. I remember emailing my wife almost daily, asking for prayer and support. I remember my integrity being challenged when I was tempted to take longer lunches or leave work early. I saw others doing it, and nothing seemed to be happening to them, which gave me even more incentive to do wrong. Yet, as bad as I felt, my back was against the wall. After all, I have a wife and four children. I was supposed to support them and *"be a man,"* right? Although I was providing for my family, I hated the way I had to provide. What was I to do?

The only choice I had was to turn to prayer and begin using the very steps I'm sharing with you in this book. God began to tenderize my heart and allow me to see what He was doing. I was able to look through those "eyes" I spoke of earlier and what I saw was God placing me among several struggling Christians who needed encouraging. These were men and women who needed my gifts. I, on the other hand, needed to grow into a man who could withstand a seemingly bad situation and remain in integrity. I needed to grow out of the man who gave thanks as long as the environment was comfortable and into someone God could trust to send wherever He needed me. As a result, I built new friendships and helped inspire new spiritual growth in others. I learned to be at peace in the midst of mayhem. I learned to be a man of integrity even when tempted by the easiest of sins.

I tell this story because of the times I've heard the testimony, "I thank God He didn't allow me to get what I wanted." Most times what we want is not what we need. Thank God, He's a father who cares more for what His children *need* than for what they want! So, thank God for all that He does. This doesn't mean you thank God for the little boy being shot last week, but it does mean you thank Him that there were no shootings this week! Learn to say thank you in all things, seeking and finding good in all God does and allows in your life.

Finally, the goal of this step is to learn how to strip ourselves of the pride and arrogance that attempts to trick us into believing our strength or education has gotten us to where we are. A great scripture to use during this time comes from the book of Deuteronomy. It reads, *"But remember the LORD your God, for it is **he who gives** you the ability to produce wealth, and so confirms his covenant, which he swore to your forefathers, as it is today."* **-Deuteronomy 8:18**

Simply say the scripture back to Him. Declare it to be true, because it is! Contrary to the foolishness we find in the world, we didn't create ourselves or give ourselves power to obtain anything. So, when we give ourselves undeserved credit, we place ourselves in serious danger of self-worship which leads to the same punishment Lucifer suffered, eternal separation from God's presence. This also hinders our ability to obey Him, because this attitude tells us that we don't need God.

So, I invite you, brothers, to take the next step towards the place we call confidence. Begin thanking God for who He is and what He does; I'm sure it will encourage you as you continue to move closer to Him. The greater our appreciation of God is, the less likely we'll be to doubt Him in the future. In fact, the more time that we spend in appreciation means that God has already done much for us, and that's something to shout about. Let's move on to our next step—praise!

How I take this step

"For everyone, this will look different, but, for me, praise sounds something like this: "Father, your word says a prudent wife is from the Lord, so I thank you for the wife you gave me. Father, your word says that children are an inheritance from the Lord, so, Father, thank you for my children. Father, your word says that you know my comings and goings, so, Father, thank you for watching over me... I just always begin by thanking Him for what is most precious to me and, from there, everything else that comes to mind. I must be honest. There is not enough time in the world for this step. Sometimes, all I do is thank Him and never get around to the other steps because I'm so overwhelmed by the memories of His grace and kindness. As you begin to spend time in praise, I'm sure you will find the same to be true for you, also."

*E*STEEM

PERSONAL THOUGHTS AND REFLECTIONS

_____

_____

_____

_____

_____

_____

_____

_____

_____

_____

_____

_____

_____

_____

_____

_____

_____

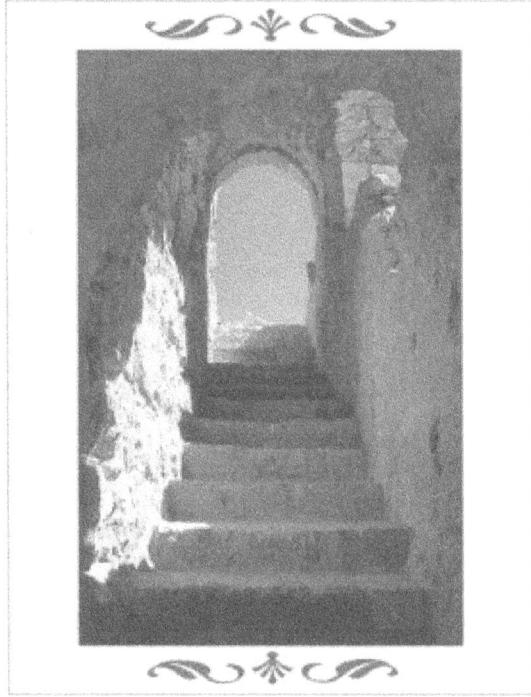

We are now ready to take the next step,
toward the place called Confidence!

Step IV
*E*xalt

*"The order of true promotion,
begins with the personal demotion of one's self!"*

Oh, yeah! Step Four is an exciting step to take! It's where we get our shout on. Now, brothers we can all relate to getting excited about something—a football game, a boxing match, anything that gets us on edge. Now, I want us to take that mindset and apply it to our time with the Lord. Brothers, let's face it. A football game is cool. A good knockout is awesome, but God is the One who gives us the ability to throw the ball or swing the punch. No matter what you get excited about, God is behind it, and, for that, He deserves our greatest praise.

What's so awesome about this step is that we're actually digging a channel to God's heart and, thus, tapping into the wellspring of life itself. So, be prepared for the river of inspiration I mentioned earlier to flow into your life. To be honest, this is my favorite step in reaching the place we call confidence, the exaltation of the Lord.

This is where we have the privilege of saying to God, "Father, you are great!" and to our challenges, "You have been overcome!" This is where we take time to promote God and demote the enemy. No matter the issue, we are able to look it in the eye and say, "In comparison to God, you have no power, authority or place in my life." When we appreciate God, we automatically deprecate our problems. The Bible instructs you and I, ***"Praise** the LORD, all his works everywhere in his dominion. **Praise** the LORD, O my soul."* **-Psalm 103:22** It is vital that we do this because it lessens the access we give to the sin and challenges in our lives. The bigger God is in our eyes, the smaller sin becomes. The more importance we put on God and time with Him, the less important other things become.

If this is your first time, or first time in a while, praising God, you are in for a real treat. Praise is so powerful that God says that He will come to where it is and make a home in it. The Bible says, *"Yet you are enthroned as the Holy One; you are the **praise** of Israel"*. **-Psalm 22:3** this is literally translated Yet you are holy, enthroned (or installed) on the praises of Israel. God honors praise so much that He created it with the power to set us free from evil. The Bible says, *"Now the Lord is the Spirit, and where the Spirit of the Lord is, **there is freedom**."* **-2nd Corinthians 3:17**

So, we can see that, where sincere, heart-felt praise is, God is. What's more is that, wherever God is, freedom is. Still, simply telling God how great He is tends to be a "roadblock" for some of us, which hinders us from developing the discipline needed to go forward in the pursuit of confidence. If we have trouble in the area of praise, we'll have trouble in every area of life. Our praising of God is directly attached to our confidence in who He is, so, until we can openly and boldly declare with our mouths that God is who He says He is and can do what He says He can do, we will continue to be hindered when He instructs us to do or say something. This sets us back because following His instruction leads to His promises being fulfilled in our lives.

For example, say you had a problem with your car, and I told you, "I can fix and repair cars." If you didn't really believe me, what's the chance you'd find me under the hood of your car this weekend?

The same applies when God tells us that He can save us from trouble or has healed us of all diseases. Although He is able to, we'll never give him the chance to work in our lives because the lack of confidence and trust prevents us from doing so. Brothers, understand something, praising God requires us to believe that He deserves to be praised and that He is who He says He is and

51

can do what He says He can do. Think of it this way. The next time your favorite player scores a winning touchdown or shoots the winning shot, take inventory of your reaction. It's likely that you'll begin shouting and praise the player for what he did; yet if we find another man worthy of our praise by simply doing his job, how much more is our Father worthy of our praise for doing His?

Another benefit of our praise is that it keeps us humble. When we spend time telling God how great He is, we begin to naturally see ourselves in need of Him. This allows us to understand that we can't live without Him. Remember when we thought we were responsible for landing that new job because of our degree or smart answers during the interview. It wasn't until we came to understand that, if it had not been for God giving us the ability to learn at those levels or the money for college or even the desire to do better in life, we would be a mess. Our praise puts God in the right perspective, which allows us to view Him as the One most deserving of recognition and adoration.

Lastly, praise allows us to enter God's presence. Remember the scripture, *"Enter his gates with thanksgiving and his courts with* **praise***; give thanks to him and* **praise** *his name."* -**Psalm 100:4** It's here that we have the privilege of completing the second instruction and experiencing the second benefit. It is through the fourth step of praise that we enter into what I like to call "the place where things are revealed," His courts. God revealed to me one day in prayer that the courts of God are where the things of God (His Word, law, blessings, revelation, healing, deliverance, etc.) are confirmed and established in a believer's life. I believe that until we learn to praise God without restraint, we have yet to truly experience God. Praise releases us from the hold of the enemy and the bondage of sin!

True, there are other steps we must take to complete our deliverance, but the process begins when we start to declare to the world that God is worthy of all praise.

There is no magic trick, no gimmick. The process is rather straightforward. We must quit fooling ourselves and think about what we once were and where we once were and decide that God deserves to be told it was only because of Him that we are better today. We all have a testimony. We all have a situation that only God could have saved us from, a situation that we know in our hearts that we did nothing to help ourselves get through. This is a great place to begin saying *"praise be"* to God!

So, go ahead and give Him the praise He deserves. Brothers, the Truth, the Way and the Life await you! Get ready to understand more than you ever have before and to experience God in ways you may not have before.

How I take this step

"This area isn't very difficult, for I know God did it all for me. When I accepted Christ, I was locked behind bars, facing 15 years for felony theft, and I know there was no way that I did anything to free myself. I was a black kid from the "hood" who robbed an affluent white man. Can we say trouble? Long story short, God made it so that the man forgave me and allowed me to be released without a scar on my record! So, I just think about situations like that and say, "My God, my God, my God, it's all because and about you!"

*E*XALT

PERSONAL THOUGHTS AND REFLECTIONS

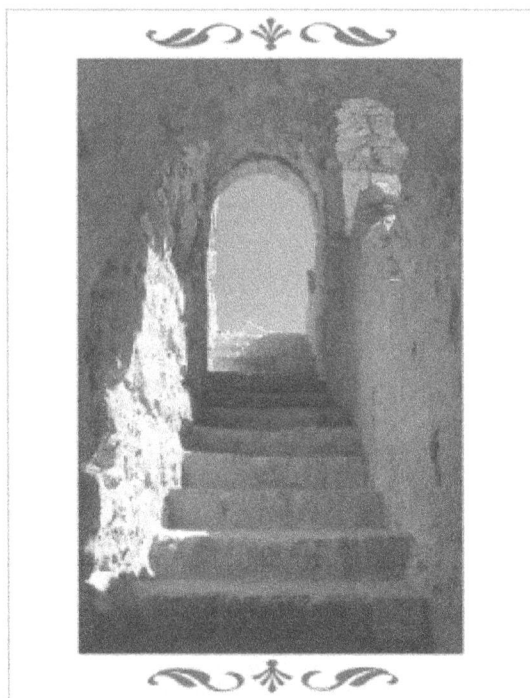

We are now ready to take the next step,
toward the place called Confidence!

Step V
*E*xpose

Before we delve into this step, allow me to share something I found absolutely profound when I first understood it. The Bible says, *"What is man that you are mindful of him, the son of man that you care for him? You made him a little lower than the heavenly beings and crowned him with glory and honor.* ***You made him ruler*** *over the works of your hands; you put* ***everything under his feet.***" **-Psalm 8: 4-6** In other words, we were created to be in control and free from every form of bondage. We are exalted above the things of the world; we are to exist in an elevated state related to all other things both physical and spiritual. Not only are we above the animals and land, but above sin, debt, guilt, shame, fear and any other form of slavery.

Freedom is a part of our DNA. We were created by God to rule and exercise dominion on the earth. When we hold our sin inside and refuse to release it to God and to others, we lock ourselves into a mental and spiritual prison that we were never meant to endure. It's self-punishment!

As we take our fifth step toward confidence, we are faced with one of our deepest fears—exposure, or the confession of our sins. The Bible says, *"This is the verdict: Light has come into the world, but men loved darkness instead of light because their* ***deeds were evil.***" **-John 3:19** Although we were originally created in spirit for freedom, our fleshly bodies have adopted a love for sin, which breeds shame and leads to bondage. No wonder fear of exposure can be overwhelming and paralyzing at times.

In order for us to fight this, brothers, we must first understand that this fear didn't come from our Father. For the Bible says, *"For God did not give us a **spirit of timidity**, but a spirit of power, of love and of self-discipline."* **-2 Timothy 1:7** Our Father is loving, caring and compassionate to his children. Through our time in prayer, He gives us the opportunity to experience the freedom that comes from His love. I have grown to appreciate this step in prayer more and more, not because of how it makes me feel, but because of how it makes me as a person. When I am able to confess my faults openly and honestly, it sends out several messages.

The first message assures God that we are serious about our desire to serve Him and be who we were created to be. The second message confirms in us, our need and trust for God. The third message informs the devil that we refuse to be condemned by him, fear, shame or guilt! The Bible says *"Therefore, there is now **no condemnation** for those who are in Christ Jesus."* - **Romans 8:1**

Listen, brothers, the mission of the enemy is to break our communion with God and alienate us with the fear of exposure, when, in fact, it is the exposure of our sin that liberates us!
Question: Have you ever done something and felt like you couldn't tell anyone and that praying would be useless because God was fed up with your mistakes? I have. I know how that feels, and it's not easy to handle. But trust me, brothers, the thing that we fear is the very thing we need most—exposure.

At this point, I'd like to offer a new perspective on coming clean. When we expose our sin, we're actually exposing the sin itself, not what we are. We are children of God. We are not sin. The sin is something we did, not what or who we are! We must not allow what we do to define who we are. We are much more than one of our acts.

At this step in our prayer, in addition to confessing all known sin, we should ask God to reveal the sins for which are unknown. The reason we need to ask God this is because we may commit *some* sins unconsciously or forget committing others all together. Remember, just because we forget about a sin doesn't mean that we don't have to address it.

For example, let's say we receive a light bill for $50, and forget to pay it, does the light company say, "Oh, they forgot to pay their bill; let's just take the charge off their account?" Of course not. In fact, if you're anything like me, there's been a time you've come home, flipped on the light switch and nothing happened, if you get my drift? Simply failing to address the issue, doesn't make it go away.

The same is true of sin. It needs to be resolved. The first step is to find out where we've missed the mark and confess. We must be honest with ourselves and others about where we are and the struggles we have. The Bible says, *"If we **confess our sins**, he is faithful and just and will forgive us our sins and purify us from all unrighteousness"* -1st **John 1:9**

Isn't this awesome of God? He loves us so much. Because He knows that we'll fall short, He creates a way for us to get right again. We don't need to wait for 30 days or jump through any hoops. No, all we need to do is let Him know we know we were wrong and that we honestly desire to do right. God responds by telling us, "I can work with that." Believe me, brothers; I've seen confession work in my own life – besides, who we foolin', we all mess up; God is just sayin' – *"Keep it real"*!

Forgiveness is a powerful thing. Forgiveness is designed to restore and refresh the soul of man. Think about the last time you honestly and completely forgave someone of their offense. Do you remember the sense of renewal and relief that came over the people who offended you when you forgave them? I believe that God created forgiveness to bring life back to the "dead" and hope back to the disheartened. What a wonderful expression and experience for those involve!

There is a release and freedom that comes from forgiveness, whether we receive it or grant it. Yet, we must address the extreme importance of forgiveness as it relates to our prayers. The Bible says, *"Therefore, if you are offering your gift at the altar and there remember that your brother has something against you, leave your gift there in front of the altar. First go and **be reconciled** to your brother; **then come** and offer your gift."*-**Matthew 5:23-24**

In other words, if we are approaching a time of prayer or sacrifice to God and realize that we and a brother aren't on good terms, we need to resolve the conflict immediately. The Bible tells us that God can't receive from us, until our brother receives from us. Elsewhere, God asks how we can love Him, whom we don't see, but hate the brothers whom we can see. If we are serious about prayer, we will be serious about forgiveness.

So, it's one thing to know that confession and forgiveness are available, but it's another to know why they are so vital to our prayer lives. In addition to helping us regain our freedom, the exposure of sin is beneficial because sin simply can't remain in the presence of God. Remember, our goal is to get to the place we call confidence. In order to get there, we must be able to remain in God's presence; un-confessed sin only hinders our time with God and prevents confidence!

God is holy, perfect, honest, clean and pure! Sin is worldly, wrong, dishonest, dirty and contaminated! Sin has to do with fear and bondage, everything God isn't. God simply will not allow it in His presence. The Bible says, *"Who may ascend the hill of the LORD? Who may stand in **his holy place**? He who has **clean hands** and a **pure heart**, who does not lift up his soul to an idol or swear by what is false."* **-Psalms 24:3-4**

God desires men of honesty and integrity to enter His presence. Holiness and sin cannot coexist. When we were born again, we were made aware of the wrongfulness of sin, yet, before salvation, we did not regret sin or fear its consequences. Now that we are in a relationship with a Holy and pure Father, we are no longer comfortable with sin. The Bible says, *"No one who is born of God will continue to sin because God's seed remains in him; **he cannot go on sinning**, because he has been born of God."* **-1st John 3:9**

Confessing and receiving forgiveness from God is the only way to truly enter His presence, and when we do, we must believe that He hears what we say. We are actually clearing the land and making room to receive the revelation we are seeking. Revelation will be covered in the steps to come, but for now, understand that un-confessed sin will always prevent us from receiving God's best because the sense of guilt makes it hard to believe we can ask God for anything.

The Bible also discusses confessing our sins to one another for the purpose of being healed. I would strongly encourage us to begin seeking another brother solid in character, prays and has the maturity in Christ to handle our confessions to serve as an accountability partner. I recommend that we pray and confirm in our hearts that the person is right for this kind of relationship. Once we have done this, we should consult this scripture: *"Therefore confess your sins to **each other** and pray for **each other** so that you may be healed. The prayer of a righteous man is powerful and effective."* **-James 5:16** and invite this brother to walk along side us.

This brings us to the last point of this step, which returns us to the goal of this book, our need for confidence. When we're able to confess our sins and know that we are forgiven, confidence is given room to begin cultivation and ultimately spring forth. Remember, what was said earlier, confidence is the key. Without it, we will never have a healthy prayer life. When we honestly believe God has forgiven us and made us clean again, we are then able to go to him and make our request with the kind of boldness He requires and desires of us. The Bible says, *"Let us then approach the throne of grace **with confidence**, so that we may receive mercy and find grace to help us in our time of need."* - **Hebrews 4:16**

Men of God, practice confession, come clean. There's no sense in playing games, God sees all things and knows us better than we know ourselves. We might as well be honest, confess what He shows us and move one step closer to the place we call confidence.

How I take this step

"I enter this step understanding that I've sinned. Rarely do I question if I've sinned, but rather where and when have I sinned. I then ask God to show me any sins I haven't identified. After this, I say, "Father you are right, and I was wrong. I understand that I am not my sin, but I have been disobedient in these areas (confess all sins openly and completely just as they were revealed), and I am sincerely sorry. I ask that you forgive me of my sin and restore me to a place of righteousness. I ask that you help me turn from sin and remain in good standing with you." From there, I usually thank Him for forgiving me and acknowledge His love for me. But my most important act is that when I've confessed sin, I move on. There is no condemnation for us in Christ, so I refuse to condemn myself."

*E*XPOSE

PERSONAL THOUGHTS AND REFLECTIONS

_____

_____

_____

_____

_____

_____

_____

_____

_____

_____

_____

_____

_____

_____

_____

_____

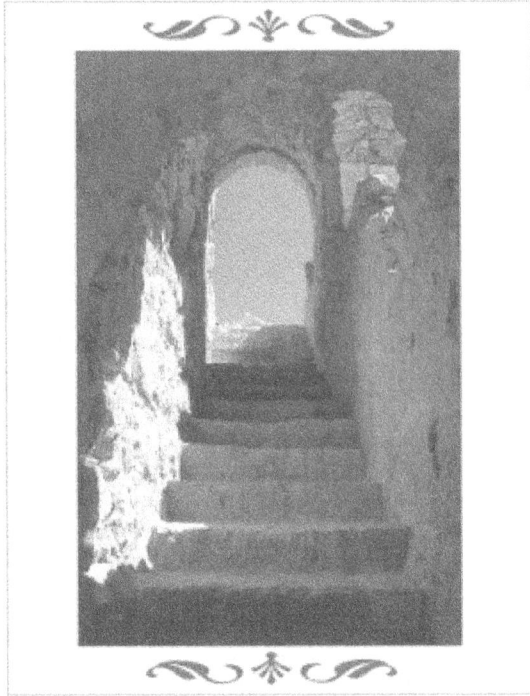

*We are now ready to take the next step,
toward the place called Confidence!*

Brothers, it's time to roll up our sleeves and dig in. Anytime we desire to grow or cultivate something, we must commit to the time and process of plowing. This is what Step Six is all about, digging in and pulling out, or extracting, from the Word of God.

What's powerful about this step is that here we transition from thinking to *knowing*. When we look at the Word of God, we come face to face with the authenticity of life, not idealism. This isn't about the misconceptions we've adopted, or the misunderstandings we've accepted. No, we are dealing with what's real—about ourselves, our lives and, most importantly, our God. It is here that we begin to pull from God's Word and acquire the conviction we need to pray with confidence. In return, we discover things in God and ourselves that we've never seen or known before.

Searching God's Word and extracting its truth is one of the most important and powerful things we can learn to do in life. The goal is for us to believe, without doubt, that what we pray for, we have. The Bible says, *"This is the confidence we have in approaching God: that if we ask anything **according to His will**, he hears us. And if we know that He hears us—whatever we ask—we know that we have what we asked of Him."* -**1st John 5:14-15**

Notice here, the Bible says this is the confidence (certainty, assurance and poise) we have. This means we have and posses a sure thing when we pray this way. What way? By His will. God's will and Word are one in the same because He and His Word are one in the same. What God wants He speaks. Our God is *the* God of integrity! He, His will and His Words align perfectly.

Brothers, God's Word can't fail. It never has, and it never will. His Word is responsible for the air we breathe and the earth we live on, for our very lives. Remember, God spoke us into existence. The Bible says, *"Then God **said**, "Let us make man in our image, in our likeness..."* **-Genesis 1:26**, God spoke! We are the evidence of the power of His Word. What more do we need?

Without God's Word in prayer, there is no confidence in prayer, because without knowing what He will approve to be granted to us, how will we have confidence in what to ask for. Hint: **GOD APPROVES HIS WORD EVERY TIME!** To think we can enter prayer without God's Word and come out with answers is like thinking we can enter a supermarket without money and come out with groceries. His Word should be taken very seriously and should be considered a prerequisite to entering a time of prayer.

The Bible says that in the beginning was the Word. Therefore, the Word has always been, and from that Word all other things came to be. As God creates, He uses his Word. And because we were created in His likeness and image (*to look, sound and act like Him*), we, too, must begin with and use His Word. The Word of God lays the foundation for all things, including our prayers. Without it, how can we truly believe that our prayers will be answered? If we don't take time to find out what God says about us and our lives, on what are we basing our prayers? How can we possibly have confidence that we will be successful in our requests?

I can't stress enough! Praying without using God's Word is like going to a bank to withdraw money without first establishing an account. How can we approach the teller with confidence? Although the bank it's self is full of money, it has no obligation to grant *us* any of it. But sadly enough, this is what we do repeatedly during prayer. We go to God asking for things we haven't confirmed in His Word and wonder why we then lack the confidence to receive it. And because we lack confidence we lack the level of faith necessary to bring the request into existence – see how one affects the other?

Take, for example, a lawyer in the process of building a case for trial. Before accepting the case, the lawyer will sit down with the parties involved and ask questions and obtain testimonies about the issue at hand. The lawyer attempts to build confidence in their clients and their ability to win the case before going to court because their integrity and career are on the line. Similarly, without the foundation of God's Word, how can we enter the courts of God and make a case for what God wants for us against the devil's claims that we don't deserve it.

Let us also, consider the construction worker. Before he builds any structure, he knows that he must first lay a strong foundation on the land. The construction worker understands that, if he doesn't begin the right way, the rest of the project will be susceptible to failure and, thus, built in vain. I once heard a building's foundation referred to as the *integrity of the structure*. Just think brothers, without a foundation of God's Word to fortify our prayers, the integrity of our requests and time with God will be weak. Brothers, we are not weak. Our prayers aren't weak, and our spirits aren't weak. We have the mind and the spirit of God working in us and for us. Let us begin to pray like it. Amen!

I encourage you to memorize 1st John 5:14-16 and remember that the confidence to approach God in prayer comes from approaching with His will as our request. I urge you to end or "seal" every prayer you pray with this scripture and verse. It will remind you that you have prayed properly and that you have a right to expect proper results! What security! To know that when we pray using God's Word we are guaranteed success!

Remember, when we take the *proper* steps to get to the place we call confidence, we will be inspired to walk closer and closer to Him, thus producing more and more confidence in Him and the future He has prepared for us to enjoy.

So, where do we begin? The best and simplest way to find the scripture that relates to our prayers is to flip to the concordance located in the back of our Bibles and look up words that are relevant to our current challenges or desires in life. A concordance lists scriptures in which the Bible's key words are mentioned. For example, if we want to develop in our faith, we want to look up one or two places where faith is mentioned in the Bible and flip to those verses. Make sure to find two or three scriptures. When beginning this process for the first time, we shouldn't worry about finding the "right" scripture. At this stage in the game, my philosophy is, if you find a scripture, you've found the right scripture! All of God's Word is good for growth and learning, at this point we can't go wrong. There'll be plenty of time for us to get into the "deeper" side of the Bible, for now, let's get what we can.

If you don't own a bible with a concordance, get one! We must be able to quickly access our artillery in times of war. I purposely did not put the word artillery in quotations because it is not a metaphor, it's REAL! The Word of God tells us "The weapons we fight with are not the weapons of the world. On the contrary, they have divine power to demolish strongholds." -2**nd** **Corinthians 10:4** The Bible also goes on to say, *"Take the* *helmet of salvation and the sword of the Spirit, which is the word* *of God."* -**Ephesians 6:17** It seems to me, we're in a fight and our weapon is God's Word!

So the problem isn't whether or not we have been given the artillery, but whether or not we choose to use it. Brothers we must take this thing seriously, the war is on and we as men have a big red target on our backs. A good solider knows where his weapons are and how to load them quickly, for he understands the importance of protecting himself and his fellow soldiers. I believe a church void of a course (*a deliberate effort*) to educate and edify its members in the process of prayer is like an army that recruits its soldiers, hands them an AK-47 and never teaches them to load it. Needless to say when *those* soldiers find themselves in the middle of warfare and oncoming fire, they will become easy targets; defenseless prey and will soon fall victim to the advancing enemy. While I remain firm in my conviction for instructional courses on prayer within every church; I have also grown to understand the responsibility of long time members to inquire of their leadership and staff for help in this area, it goes both ways.

So as we continue through this corridor never lose sight of the fact that we are in a war, a war being fought for our lives. The enemy will attempt to distract us by insisting the Bible is too big for this exercise, so we should just forget it. The enemy will also attempt to discourage us if we're unable to locate a word we're looking for in the concordance. If this happens, return to the second step of esteeming and being thankful that we're even in His Word. I'd also advise us to contact a brother or Pastor from our church and invite them to help us locate what we need. This will not only infuriate Satan, but position us to receive twice the blessing! The Bible says, *"And without faith it is impossible to please God, because anyone who comes to him must believe that he exists and that he **rewards those** who earnestly **seek him**."* - **Hebrews 11:6.** Not only will we receive what we're looking for in the Word, but also receive rewards from God for our diligence.

So, whether or not we find the word that we are looking for at that moment, understand that He will reward an honest effort. Be encouraged. God can be relied upon to bring people into our lives to help us study His Word. If we still do not find the scripture we are looking for, turn to any chapter in Psalms and Proverbs, for these books address a range of troubles and challenges that come a believer's way.

Be assured that when we consult the Bible for understanding, God paves the way to enlightenment. We will read scripture that makes sense to our spirits even if we don't have an intellectual understanding of the scripture yet. The Bible speaks of our spirits testifying with His spirit because we are His children. Surely, God will speak to His children in a way that they can understand. There will be a connection even if it doesn't feel like it initially.

Finally brothers, I want to share perhaps the most important aspect of extracting God's Word for our time in prayer— faith. Faith is the juice of life; faith is the gasoline in the tank of the vehicle we call prayer. Again I refuse to use quotations here, because prayer literally takes us from one place to another, most often from *dis*couragement to *en*couragement! Let's take a look at this more closely.

The Word of God says, *"Is any one of you sick? He should call the elders of the church to pray over him and anoint him with oil in the name of the Lord. And the prayer **offered in faith** will make the sick person well; the Lord will raise him up. If he has sinned, he will be forgiven. Therefore confess your sins to each other and pray for each other so that you may be healed. The prayer of a righteous man is powerful and effective."-* **James 5:14-16** Notice the scripture implies not just any prayer will work, but rather the prayer offered in (faith) will make the sick person well. This is important to understand if our desire is to pray with confidence, because faith is directly connected to our level of *confidence* in prayer.

It is faith that charged this prayer with power, it is faith that makes the prayer of the righteous man powerful and effective and will do the same for us today. The key is first understanding what faith is.

The Bible says *"Now faith is **being sure** of what we hope for and **certain of** what we do not see. This is what the ancients were commended for. By faith **we understand** that the universe was formed at God's command, so that what is seen was not made out of what was visible."* - **Hebrews 11:1-3** According to this passage, faith is certainty, belief and assurance. I don't know about you, but, it looks to me that faith and confidence not only are similar but are the same. So with this understanding, we could say without difficulty, the prayer offered in *confidence* (faith) will make the sick person well.

Before I continue, I want to stop and make a point I believe is vital for us to grasp; biblical faith and earthly confidence are not one in the same. Earthly confidence is built on *people's* ability, biblical confidence or faith, is built on *God's* ability. Just because someone has a (natural) earthly confidence in their ability or that of others, doesn't equal success. But a man with biblical confidence, *(faith in what God can do)*, is guaranteed success in his request.

I know what you're saying, nothing in life is guaranteed. You may even be asking, how I can be so sure that our prayers will be successful? To answer this question let us return to the passage we began this step with, 1st John 5:14-15. This passage guarantees us that if we pray (ask) anything according to God's will (which is His Word) He hears us and because He hears us, we have it! The confidence we are using for our prayers is completely based on the Word of God, period. As stated earlier, God and His Word are one in the same, which means, His Word can't fail, for if His Word was to fail, He would fail, and that's not possible. In fact, God has placed such a high demand on his Word that His very name and character are on the line.

Any man worthy of being called a man knows his name and his word are all he really has in life, for these two things help shape his character and character proceeds all else! Either he will be known as a man trustworthy and respectable, or immoral and disreputable. Our name and our word will either make or break us in life. The level of integrity in which people associate our name and word will determine our progress with every facet of life.

The Bible says, "*I will bow down toward your holy temple and will praise your name for your love and your faithfulness, for you have exalted **above all things** your name and your word*". - **Psalm 138:2** God has exalted above everything, His name and His Word. What this passage says to me is, God has placed more significance on His name and Word than anything else, and will not defy them. In short, God obeys His Word.

WOW, what a powerful revelation and confidence we're able to walk in, knowing the One that created Heaven and Earth, will obey His Word and that He has given us permission to use it everyday of our lives! Brothers, the bottom line is that, without a word from God, we will be fruitless in our attempts to reach a place of confidence in prayer or any where else for that matter!

Today let us open our Bibles and find a word to meditate on and trust in, knowing that we have what is necessary to receive what we seek in prayer. Make sure that there is plenty of His Word to meditate on because Step Seven requires us to turn to the scriptures we have gathered here.

How I take this step

"I approach this step by thinking of what the needs and concerns in my life and my loved ones' lives are. I then ask God to lead me to scriptures that will relate to these things. I usually write down the scripture or put a book mark on the page where it is found. I read the scripture repeatedly until I start to see and understand matters on a deeper level. Once I get a greater understanding, I say aloud what I hear in my head. Next, I repeat the scripture out loud and thank God for my revelation. I keep in mind what I have learned as I enter Step Seven."

*E*XTRACT

PERSONAL THOUGHTS AND REFLECTIONS

_____

_____

_____

_____

_____

_____

_____

_____

_____

_____

_____

_____

_____

_____

_____

_____

We are now ready to take the next step,
toward the place called Confidence!

Step VII
*E*stablish

In Step Seven, we come into a time of declaration and prophecy—the establishment of God's Word for our lives. Although God's Word is given to us and is for our benefit, we must establish it in faith and deed. Now that we have read His Word, gathered the proof of our promises and developed the conviction to hold on to them, we can boldly approach His throne. The reason it's so important to read and lay a foundation based on His Word before we place our requests before God is to establish confidence.

Remember the example of the construction worker. Before construction workers or building contractors start a project, they survey the land to determine if there is good ground to build on. In our case, the land or ground is represented by our hearts. The heart is the very center of a man, his core and mind. What a man does or says first begins in his heart, and then flows into his life. In Step Five, we addressed this, so we're prepared for the foundation to be laid. The foundation is vitally important to the builder because he knows that, if it is strong, the entire building will stand. If it is weak, however, it will fall. Brothers, be encouraged, when we acquire God's Word, we lay the strongest foundation possible.

In Step Six, we learned how to extract from God's Word. Here, we will utilize what we've extracted and establish it for our lives. Brothers, read the following sentence carefully: Many people struggle in the area of prayer because they lack the confidence necessary to believe that God hears them, and, to some degree, they're right. I don't say this to be discouraging, but to be direct. God hears and listens to the truth. Below are scriptures that address what we can do to ensure that God hears our prayers.

The Bible says, *"In the beginning was the Word, and the Word was with God, and the **Word** was God."* **-John 1:1** It also says, *"Sanctify them by the truth; your **word is truth**."* **-John 17:17**.

Lastly, the scriptures say, *"Yet a time is coming and has now come when the true worshipers will worship the Father in spirit and **truth**, for they are the kind of worshipers the Father seeks."* **-John 4:23**. So, we understand that God desires for people to worship Him (*say, think and act*) in line with His word. If we are making requests in prayer that are not based on God's Word, we will not be heard.

The Bible says, *"**If** my people, who are called by my name, will humble themselves and pray and seek my face and turn from their wicked ways, then will I hear from heaven and will forgive their sin and will heal their land."* **-2 Chronicles 7:14**

There are guidelines to obtaining God's attention. We began this process by listing our expectations, the things we believe God can and will do for us. Be it His presence, His blessing or His confidence, we are seeking God's involvement in our lives. This is important to understand because prayer should not be seen as just going through the motions. If we view it that way, we will be doing just that—moving a lot and going nowhere.

So, let's be honest, we need God to hear us. If you pick up your phone to ask for your friend's help, yet you never dial the number, how likely is it that your friend heard you? How confident can you be that your friend will come to your aid? Seems silly, right? Well, the same is true for us, as it concerns prayer. God's number is **1-800-HIS-WORD**, and, unless we dial that number, we can't expect Him to hear our requests. Remember, when He hears us, we have the confidence to know we have what we ask for. It doesn't get any simpler than that. If He hears us, we have it, yet how we get Him to hear us is our response-*ability*! And our responsibility is searching His word and praying according to the word we find.

Brothers, please understand that it's not that God doesn't want to hear us when we pray. It's that he can't hear us. The use of the word "hear" in this context does not refer to the ability to hear audible sound but the ability to agree or respond to what is being said. It's similar to asking your friend if he "feels" you, or turning to someone and saying, *"you know what I'm sayin"*. You know your friend can hear you talking, the point is, you're looking for their *agreement* in what you're saying. The same is true of God. God hears us audibly every time we open our mouths. The problem has been for many of us, we are attempting to get God's involvement in our lives without seeking His agreement.

Have you, for example, encountered a voice activation system? Maybe you've called a business and an automated system answered and began walking you through several commands that required certain responses as you moved through the menu of choices.

Question: What happened when you didn't give responses with the tone and clarity required by the automated system? You made no progress, right? The system simply waited for you to give the proper response in the proper tone. It's not that it doesn't hear what you say. In fact, in some cases, the machine will ask for you to repeat yourself, which indicates that it hears you but can't allow you to progress until you provide the answer it seeks.

Now, I'm not saying that God is some cold-blooded machine that sits there all day waiting for us to give the right response before He helps us, but He does speak in the language of truth. Truth activates God! When God hears truth (His Word) coming from us, His heart is moved to action! This is why we have taken the steps to expose, or be truthful about, our sins and why we begin prayer with thanksgiving and praise. In doing so, we are being truthful about our need for God and how great He is. This step is no different. God requires truth in our communion with Him.

So, how does this step really look?

First, we want to begin by acknowledging that we're in His presence! Take a moment and express gratitude that God not only allows us in to fellowship with Him, but He also shows us how to get to that step. Have you ever had someone tell you to do something without first showing you how to do it? If so, you know the frustration that can result from that, so we should be thankful that our Father isn't that way!

Secondly, we want to ask God to lead our prayer. This is important because we don't always know what to pray for. Even though we have our scriptures and expectations, there are sometimes unseen obstacles (natural and supernatural) that we may not be aware of, but God is and will direct us to pray about them, allowing us to have our expectations and requests met.

It's important to note that this step not only applies to us personally but also to our efforts to intercede for others. As names and faces of loved ones surface, God should be called upon to lead prayers according to His will for their lives. This step is powerful because, as people ask us to pray for them, God will lead us to their needs and not only their wants, allowing us to really have an impact on their lives. They will know we prayed for them because things will happen in their lives that lead to substantial change!

Now, let's put this step to work.

In Step Six, we extracted scriptures that we will now consult. Open your Bible to the scriptures we gathered and pray based on what they say. For example, we have an issue to address which requires wisdom. Before we pray, we decide to use James 1:5, which states, *"If any of you lacks wisdom he should ask God ..."* So, we read that scripture out loud and then saying to God in prayer, "God, according to Your Word, that says, If any of you lacks wisdom, he should ask God, who gives generously to all without finding fault, and it will be given to him. Father I am asking for Wisdom; God give me the wisdom I need to handle this situation in my life. And Father, your Word also says in, **1st John** 5:14-15, *"This is the confidence we have in approaching God: that if we ask anything **according to His will**, He hears us. And if we know that He hears us—whatever we ask—we know that we have what we asked of Him"*. Because the scriptures say this, I know that you hear me. I make this request according to and based on your Word. So, I declare that I have wisdom to handle this situation in my life, thank you God, Amen!"

You Got It!

We have just prayed with confidence and are assured an answer from God. It's important here to apply the faith we spoke of in our last chapter to our request. Remember it is the faith in knowing what God says about the situation that super charges our prayers and cause them to become powerful and effective. Don't doubt or look for a feeling. Too often we wait for a feeling or some spooky thing to happen to prove to us that our prayer has been answered, but God doesn't work that way. In fact, the Bible warns us in the scripture we just used not to doubt, or else we shouldn't believe we will receive anything from God. God is surely in agreement with His Word, for He is His Word. He doesn't waiver or falter. If He did, He would fail to be Himself and that can't happen.

We must believe He *has* delivered! The reason I use the word *has* here is because God's Word can't fail and because it can't fail, what He says is already done – *already*! He's simply waiting for us to agree with His Word. He's waiting for us to make requests that align with His Word and plan for our lives. This should be our goal with every prayer! We want to base it on what we know about the Word of God, not what we think is a good idea or what we were told the other night at Bible study. Trust me, the Bible covers every issue, struggle and situation we can have or find ourselves in. Search the Bible for it and use it to pray for God's will, and watch things start to change!

A final point I'd like to make is to be you! In our time with God, we are free to ask and even vent as needed. We've reached Him and He welcomes us with open arms. We don't need to speak in King James English or remember all the steps to this book. Just enjoy the fact that God accepts us as we are. When we come with all the pains, all the hurts, all the junk, He says, "Give all that to me. I'll handle it for you." As with any good Father, God is compassionate and enjoys time with His children. We can count on Him to use this time to tell us things we never thought we would hear and show us things we never could have imagined. He will allow us to experience Him in ways we never have before!

What we request and receive will vary from time to time, but the processes never do. Remember this is a book created, not to tell us what to say, but simply to provide the order in which to say it. We may be entering a time of intercession for others or a time for ourselves where we lay our needs before the Lord. Either way, we should always ask God to lead us as we enter this time with Him.

How I take this step

"Before I gratefully enter this time, I acknowledge the fact that I'm in God's presence and that I am privileged to be able to make requests of my Father. I then ask God to lead me in prayers for myself and for others, because, again, I think I know what I want, but the lack of what I need is preventing me from obtaining it. And, lastly, I focus on the scriptures I've found. The Word can't fail, so what better place to spend the bulk of my time in this step than prophesying back to God and the world what I know is true, His Word!"

*E*STABLISH

PERSONAL THOUGHTS AND REFLECTIONS

_____

_____

_____

_____

_____

_____

_____

_____

_____

_____

_____

_____

_____

_____

_____

_____

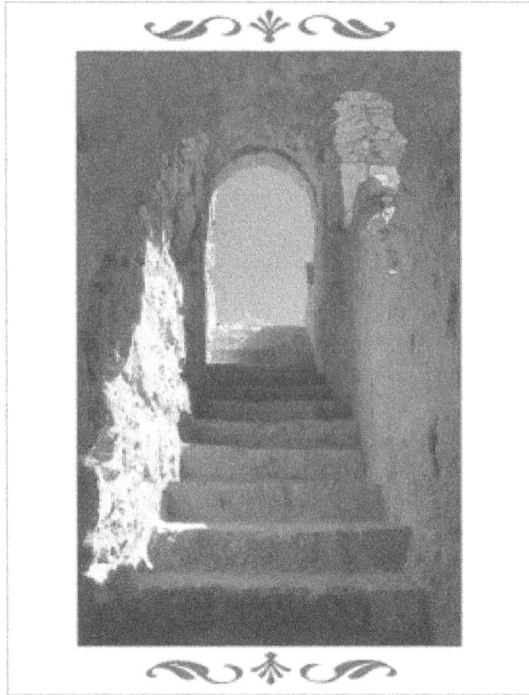

We are now ready to take the next step,
toward the place called Confidence!

Step VIII
*E*dify

A favorite saying of mine is: "*You can't take someone somewhere you haven't first been yourself.*" In other words, if you haven't been there before, how can you show me the way? In this step we'll be taking the eighth step toward the place we call confidence, the edifying, or *building up*, of ourselves.

Those without a clue call this step selfish. Others honestly don't know its importance, but, before we leave prayer and re-enter the cold cruel world that we live in, we better get grounded. And for those of us who want to "save the world for Christ", we must first be saved ourselves.

For example, a man who grows up with self-esteem issues and a low self-image will find it difficult to tell other men how great *they* are, until that man first gains a sense of self-worth for himself; otherwise, he will continue to see life and other men based on how he see himself. My pastor and spiritual father, Kerwin Manning, first taught me that "*hurt people; hurt people*". In other words, we who are wounded will likely wound others and will relate to others through self-reflection until our mind and concept of ourselves are changed by the Word of God!

Think. Who knows you better than you, besides God Himself? You know where you are in life. You know how you feel about yourself. I have heard it said that we can't give what we don't have. That's like asking a man with no car for a ride to work. He's not able! So, before you head out to fight the "*good fight of faith*" put some armor on, get built up, change the way you see yourself, and get battle *ready*. Remember, we're in a war and the battlefield is our mind. Our thoughts are connected to and dictate everything else we say and do. Our thoughts about ourselves must be in line with God's Word concerning us and others, before we can enter this fight with confidence. Remember, confidence is vital to our prayers; it's what causes us to fight and *continue* fighting.

At this step we want to open our Bibles and gather scriptures that tell us who we are in the Lord. We must find at least two to three scriptures that speak to us directly, that tell us that we are more than what the world tells us we are. The Bible speaks of things being established on the testimony of two and three witnesses, I figure why not gather two to three testimonies from the scriptures to use here. Here are a few you may want to use to get started.

<u>We are co-heirs of glory, heavenly and earthly.</u>

*"Now if we are children, then we are heirs—heirs of God **and co-heirs** with Christ, if indeed we share in his sufferings in order that we may also share in his glory".*
-Romans 8:17

<u>We are the righteousness of God.</u>

*"God made him who had no sin to be sin for us, so that in Him we might become the **righteousness** of God".*
-2 Corinthians 5:21

<u>We are world over-comers.</u>

*"Who is it that **overcomes** the world? Only he who believes that Jesus is the Son of God".*
-1 John 5:5

Has anyone ever told you something about yourself that felt awesome, yet unbelievable at the same time? I have. I recall the first time I was told that I was a teacher of the gospel. A dear brother in the Lord named Eric Brown, who has since passed away, told me this following a small men's meeting at which I shared a brief message from the Book of Matthew. Pastor Eric simply walked up to me, leaned into my ear and said, *"You're a teacher."* He then looked me in the eye, smiled and walked away. Man, I was on cloud nine for about three days, but then the feeling faded, and I began to doubt myself and over think the compliment. Later however, I was edified and became convinced when more brothers began to confirm this word in me by walking up and saying the same thing. Today, I am completely confident that God has called me to teach His Word. It just took a consistent flow of *witnesses* to remind me.

We also want to take the scriptures we've gathered and boldly confess them over ourselves and back to God. Read them aloud, put music to them, or even shout them. It doesn't matter how we do it, as long as we rejoice in them and get excited. It's all true, and it's all about us. This is why some believe this step causes arrogance and is unnecessary. But, please, if God said it about us, we better say it about us. I have faith that when we pray the right way, we are humble in spirit and can receive this kind of honor. When I do this step, I love to walk around the room with my Bible in hand and read line after line. Then, I take each line of those scriptures and make them personal, putting my name in eac sentence.

For example, let's use one from earlier, the Bible says, **"God** *made him who had no sin to be sin for us, so that in Him **we** might become the **righteousness** of God."* **-2 Corinthians 5:21** we then can say, *"According to 2 Corinthians 5:21, in agreement with your Word, I declare, I, (your name here), have become the righteousness of God. I am the righteousness of God. I am your righteous today!"*

Brothers, as we listen to ourselves say the same things God says about us and reflect on them repeatedly, we are changed from the inside. What happens is we begin to replace the negative, self-demoralizing, disheartening mind set we've developed over the course of our lives with the truth of the One who created us. This is why the devil attempts to manipulate the Word of God and convince churchgoers to view this process as ungodly because it exposes the truth about us, the last thing the devil wants us to know.

This is another difficult area for men in prayer because, again, it deals with the Word of God. Anytime we go directly to the Word, we will get the uncut truth. I believe the reason the devil fights so hard to discourage us from this step is because of his mission. The Bible says that he comes to steal, kill and destroy (our identity in Christ). If we learn who we *really* are and what we *really* can do, we will begin to demand more of ourselves and experience the victory that has been given to us.

Lastly, the greatest benefit to this step is the perspective we gain for others. Remember how we see ourselves is how we see others. The more we understand what God has put in us, the more we accept that He did it for others as well. So, as we prepare to pray for others, we will see them in the proper light. By seeing ourselves as God does, we will begin to speak the same life-building scriptures over others, which makes God very pleased and allows Him to intervene and bring them to a place where they, too, can stand.

When we build ourselves up in the Lord with a sincere and humble heart, we are actually building up the natural and spiritual seed within us, as well as everyone connected to us. Remember we can only give away what we first obtain ourselves!

How I take this step

"The Bible is stocked with scripture that tells us how much God loves us. I don't get really specific in my choice of scripture unless I am faced with a challenge that requires me to see myself in a certain way to overcome it. Generally, I search familiar passages and remind myself who I really am. Then, I allow God to lead me to more scriptures. As I find them, I declare them to be true and speak of myself in relation to the scriptures. If they speak of something I haven't experienced yet, I remember Romans 4:17 and call things that are not as if they were. I remember that everything starts with a word. If I don't release a word, how can it ever become a reality?"

*E*DIFY

PERSONAL THOUGHTS AND REFLECTIONS

_____

_____

_____

_____

_____

_____

_____

_____

_____

_____

_____

_____

_____

_____

_____

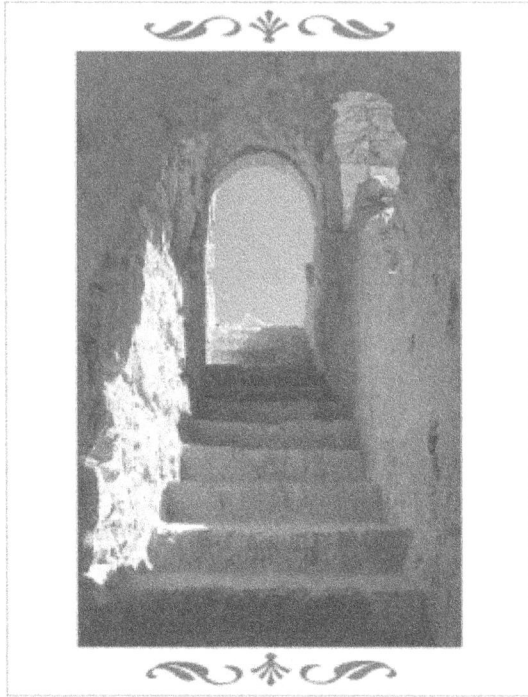

We are now ready to take the next step,
toward the place called Confidence!

Step IX
*E*xit

The Bible says, *"Then Jesus told his disciples a parable to show them that they should always pray and **not give up**."* **-Luke 18:1** In this passage, Jesus gives His disciples a bit of a "pep talk." As Jesus goes on, he reveals the necessity and benefit of praying, or making *consistent*, heartfelt requests before God. Results are produced by never giving in or giving up.

Elsewhere in the Bible, God indicates that it is His will for us to pray without stopping. *"Be joyful always; **pray continually**; give thanks in all circumstances, for this is God's will for you in Christ Jesus.,"* states **-1 Thessalonians 5:16-18.**

Yet, in terms of bringing a structured prayer to an end, there is a process. The ninth step to reaching a place of confidence in prayer charts how to effectively exit a time of prayer.

First, it is important that we exit our time of prayer attentively. As we leave a personal, structured time of prayer, we should remain in a prayerful, or meditative, state. For years I wondered, how am I supposed to pray continually? Was it really expected of me to pray all day? What about errands, work and family? Then, I realized the way to pray unceasingly is to remain conscious of God's presence throughout the day and be willing to be used by God at any moment and/or pray for others.

In Step Seven, we learned that communion with God is great. Now, we see that communion never has to end. God desires continual unity with us. We can go about our day, thinking about God, singing songs that draw us closer to God and His Word. We can also take little prayer breaks in the middle of the day. How to structure these breaks is up to you. Be creative, and remember that, what may work for another, may not work for you, so find what's right for you and do it!

The reason it is important to remain in communion with God continuously is because things will come up throughout the day that require His help. If we remain in a steady state of communion, we will likely be ready to participate in what God is doing in our own as well as in other people's lives.

We should also exit a time of prayer with confidence; as we have made a huge investment at this point. We began by learning what prayer is and why we need to pray. We then learned to expect great things from God and eliminate distractions from our time with Him. We went on to esteem God for who and what He is to us. We've exalted God's name and reminded ourselves of all the great things He has done through us. We've exposed the sin in our lives. We've entered His presence. We've extracted the truth of God's Word and positioned ourselves to receive revelation. Lastly, we've edified ourselves by God's Word that we may stand strong and bold in the fight.

It would make no sense to accomplish all of this and doubt that victory is on the way. When we explored edification, it was to prepare us not to faint. The Bible says, *"Do you not know that in a race all the runners run, but only one gets the prize?* **Run in such a way** *as to get the prize."* **-1 Corinthians 9:24** In other words, in life we must learn to pace ourselves. We have to understand that prayer, like anything else worth doing, requires endurance. Actually, this step shouldn't be called exiting at all. It's more like entering a new level, or stage, of prayer, for the morning prayer with which we begin our day should actually serve as a prelude to a day, week or lifestyle of *continual* prayer.

The more we fall in love with spending time with God, the sooner we'll discover that we can't stay away from prayer. God will consume us in a way that keeps us aware of His presence and love all day long. The Bible says *"Taste and see that the Lord is good, that blessed is the man who takes refuge in him"*- **Psalm 34:8** While this doesn't mean to literally taste as with our tongue, it does however illustrate perfectly how good time with God is; it's like having seconds of your favorite food.

It is my hope and prayer that you don't fight this step. Instead, allow God to consume you and move you to new levels of intimacy with Him. Give yourself permission to explore prayer and be open to seeing it in a new way. Challenge yourself to go deeper. Aren't you a little curious about what it's like to spend the whole day with God, to feel the same peace and comfort you did when you prayed this morning? Experiencing an ongoing, never ending relationship with our Father is why we were created. Remember that when God met Adam in the cool of day, He was delighted to see and be with Adam. Allow God to take delight in His time with you. Follow this step and watch Him do amazing things in your life.

How I take this step

As I depart from my time of structured prayer, I think about God and how much He has done for me and through me. I spend the bulk of my day recalling scripture. Sometimes, I am reminded of the miserable life I led before Christ entered my life. During these moments, I like to share how God has transformed my life with others. The Word of God says, "The Spirit himself testifies with our spirit that we are God's children." **-Romans 8:16** *And whenever this happens to me, I allow my spirit's testimony to come out of my mouth. I can't get enough of it. I have no doubt that once you arrive at this step, you won't be able to get enough of it either. I want to be able to say, "I have fought the good fight, I have finished the race, I have kept the faith."* **-2 Timothy 4:7.** *Don't you?*

*E*XIT

PERSONAL THOUGHTS AND REFLECTIONS

_____

_____

_____

_____

_____

_____

_____

_____

_____

_____

_____

_____

_____

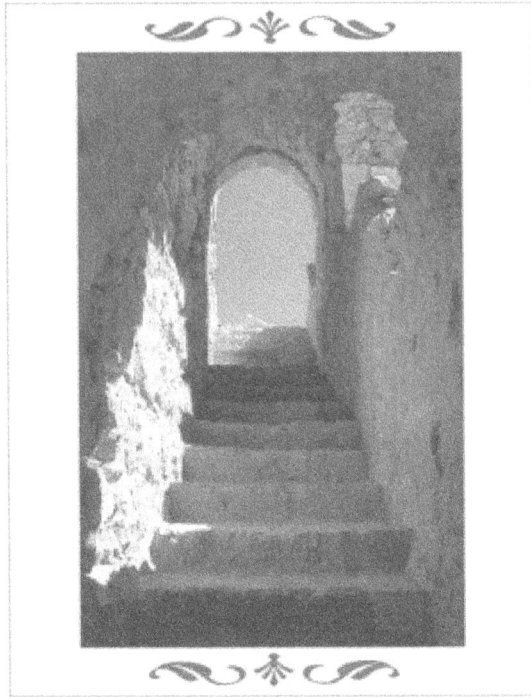

We are now ready to take the next step,
toward the place called Confidence!

Step X
*E*xecute

Goals and Accomplishments:
"Effort you don't want to give & Time you don't think you have"

Now that you have prayed structurally and begun to pray continually, the next and, perhaps, most vital step is to execute! We do this by acting on our beliefs. Someone once wrote, "The definition of insanity is to do the same things over and over and expect different results." Brothers, we're not insane, in fact we've been given the mind of Christ! So we can say with confidence, we will adapt accordingly and *do* what is necessary to receive new and powerful results.

We learned in step nine that we must remain in a prayerful state and in communion with God throughout the day. Our ability to hear the voice of God is absolutely important and should be taken very seriously. The reason for this is because obedience leads to promise. If we can't hear God's directions, how will we ever reach the place he desires for us to be? We must understand that our ability to *obey* the voice of God depends on our ability to *hear* the voice of God. Breaking our time of communion can cause us to miss opportunities to execute (do God's Word), and as a result, miss the promise (the answer we prayed for).

Some time ago, I faced a dilemma at work that required me to obey God and execute his Word. I had arrived to work 90 minutes early, and, as the day drew to a close, I became very tired. Several minutes before I was scheduled to leave, I packed up my belongings and headed out the door. I reasoned to myself that I hadn't taken a lunch, so leaving early would make a difference. But as I stepped into the elevator, I began to ponder my decision. I could sense God prompting in my heart a question – *"How could you remain a man of integrity and cheat my boss out of time"*? However, like many of us do, I began to contemplate the voice I heard, yet continued to move closer to my car. I actually managed to climb into my car but as soon as I did, the Lord reminded me of a passage I read earlier that week in prayer with my pastor. *"The LORD is **righteous** in all his ways and loving toward all he has made"*-**Psalm 145:17** I recalled when I first read this, how excited I was and how I declared that I would strive to be *righteous* in all my ways as the Lord is. After all, God created me to be like him! As I considered my situation, I thought – "Here's my chance to do so, here's my chance to execute"!

With literally minutes left, I figured there was no sense in actually walking all the way back to my office, but I *could* refrain from leaving early by remaining in the parking lot until my day was finished. This may sound extreme or unreasonable, but to obtain God's promises, we must be willing to correct ourselves and do the unreasonable. In the time that I had remaining, I began worshiping God and thanking Him for holding me to a higher standard. I share this in light of being a salaried employee, which means by company standards, leaving early carries no weight on my work day hours or pay. However, as a child of God, my standards are not those of my employer, *but of God*.

While I was worshiping, I heard a loud crash outside of the parking lot just as the clock struck 4 p.m. – *the end of my shift*. As I pulled up the ramp and out of the lot I discover there had been an accident directly in front of my office building. Had I decided to ignore God's voice and leave a few minutes early that day, I could have been involved in that accident. Nevertheless because I remained prayerful throughout my day, I was open to correction by the Holy Spirit, able to hear God's voice and avoided danger.

So, let's not waste time. Let's prepare ourselves now to execute, knowing that when we do, we will move closer to obtaining complete confidence in God!

Another aspect of the execution step is to look for ways to act on what you prayed! A few years ago, I joined a large company that provided weekend trainings. During these trainings, we spent several hours learning about the company's benefits and procedures, including how to market and grow the company, increase sales and build our workforce. Because the managers understood that it was important to build people up and prepare them for the week ahead, much praise and recognition was given during the trainings as well. The goal was to build up our confidence and deepen our conviction in the company.

At the end of every training session, the managers would say, "Now, don't wait; go out right now and put this into practice right away!" They understood that, if we waited, it was likely we would lose heart and be prone to "drag butt" during that week. They wanted us to go out and execute what we learned right away, so we could see results immediately and thus, grow in confidence.

The same is true for us in the area of prayer. When we get off our knees and head out for the day armed with the power that prayer gives us, God prepares ways for us to live out His Word. We won't need to look long before life presents us with an opportunity to execute on what we've asked for or heard in prayer. Though, it's important to note that when we pray correctly, the devil will begin to challenge our authority. This shouldn't frighten us, for God has empowered us to experience success in all matters executed under *His* direction. So, just go for it and know that God is with you!

The importance of execution can't be stressed enough because, when we fail to execute, we lose a sense of who we are. The Bible says, *"Do not merely listen to the word, and so deceive yourselves. Do what it says. Anyone who listens to the word but does not do what it says is like a man, who looks at his face in a mirror and, after looking at himself, goes away and immediately forgets what he looks like."* **-James 1:22-23** In short, he thoughtfully observes himself just to go off and forget what he was like.

As it relates to prayer, this would mean that, after praying and receiving God's direction for our lives, we leave and fail to execute what we know to do, which means we failed to believe God's Word. Understand however, that while we may fail in certain moments, we are not failures. We are not our actions. We are children of God. That being said, we can't allow our failure to execute to define us as men. Instead, we must remain aware of God's grace, tell Him our fears, expose them and ask for the courage and wisdom to do better next time. God speaks the language of truth, so, when we, in turn, speak in truth, He will hear us and help us to succeed in the future.

When we succeed in executing our prayers, we begin to see ourselves as God does and build a stronger kingdom for Him. It is helpful to remind ourselves that victory is not only in our faith, but in acting on faith when fear challenges us to shrink back and not execute. The Bible says, *"As the body without the spirit is dead, so faith without **deeds** is dead."* -**James 2:26** Think of an athlete who trains for several months just to fold his arms and sit down on race day. How will the athlete ever know the taste of victory if he fails to execute what he's been trained to do?

This leads us back to the company I spoke of earlier. The company had several philosophies, including the practice of disconnecting from the outcome. Such a philosophy is especially important in the world we live in today, where image is everything and the way we look to others seems to outweigh how we look to ourselves. The truth is that we sometimes put too much emphasis on the outcome we desire. When we invest in the outcomes we believe should occur, we tend to forget that God has a bigger plan and final say in what should and shouldn't be. Why is keeping this in mind so vital to our prayer lives? It's vital because this behavior allows fear (which doesn't come from God) to prevent us from moving to the next step in our prayer lives: experience.

Questions to Consider

- If I never execute what I learned in prayer, what was the point of praying?"
- If I never act, or execute, when I hear God's voice, what is preventing me from doing so?
- If I never execute, how can I expect anything in my life to change?

We entered our time of prayer with the expectation to be inspired. And when inspired, we should act on or execute based on what we were given. God gives us knowledge, wisdom, insight and power, so we can achieve great things. Brothers, we can spend hours praying and crying out to God every day, but if we are not willing to execute His plans, we will continue to fall short and lack confidence.

I think this is a great time to pause and draw from the wisdom and truthfulness of this popular saying: "If you do what you've always done, you'll get what you've always gotten."

Whether we realize it or not, when God moves, He moves through people. There has never been a breakthrough, harvest or any form of blessing that God granted me that didn't come through a man or woman. When God uses His children to help others, He knows that not only will He be glorified, but that we are built up as well. When we execute, we experience the fullness of God's power, which fosters confidence in us.

In summary, if we don't execute, how can God use us to do His works? God will not always call on us to act, but if we are unwilling when the time comes, how great is our confidence? When we're given the opportunity to execute, our level of confidence is revealed. We must be confident that God's Word is true and that we have received what we need during prayer. If we are lacking in this area, we will never experience God's vision for our lives. So, don't wait to act. Now is the time to execute. God's given us the ability, so take advantage of it and move from being a thinker to being a knower.

How I take this step

"I execute by maintaining a mindset of victory. I remind myself repeatedly of God's Word, remembering that He can never fail. So, if He gives me a command, I obey it. I also remember to disconnect myself from the results. God tells us what to do in a situation, but He doesn't always reveal what the result of his commands will be. At times, I have decided what I think the outcome of a situation should be, forgetting that God sees all things and knows the outcome. Our focus should remain on obedience to the Word, not on fear of the outcome!"

*E*XECUTE

PERSONAL THOUGHTS AND REFLECTIONS

_____

_____

_____

_____

_____

_____

_____

_____

_____

_____

_____

_____

_____

_____

_____

_____

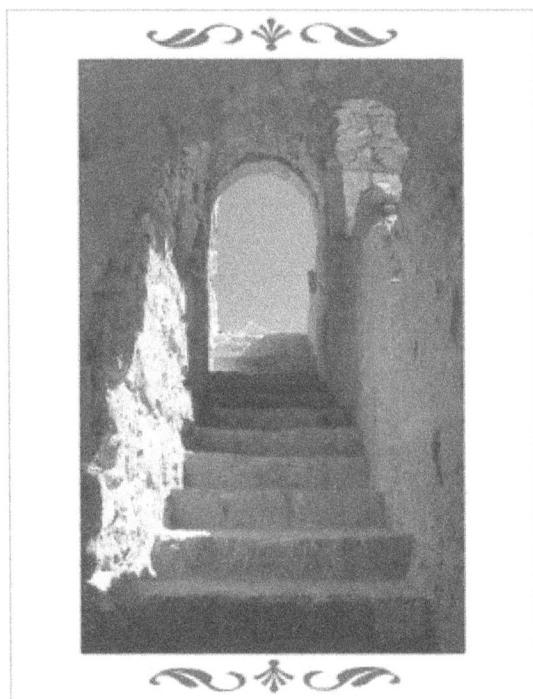

We are now ready to take the next step,
toward the place called Confidence!

"Life begins at I can"

This step will serve as a training ground of sorts on how to achieve *complete* confidence in prayer! This is an important step of increasing our confidence for several reasons, which are discussed throughout this chapter.

An experience has more to do with results and reflections than with actual prayer, for it is a result of our execution. When we pray correctly and execute obediently, we experience God's power and credit Him with what manifests in our lives.

The Bible says, *"Praise the LORD, O my soul; all my inmost being, praise His holy name. Praise the LORD, O my soul, and* **forget not all His benefits**—*who forgives all your sins and heals all your diseases, who redeems your life from the pit and crowns you with love and compassion, who satisfies your desires with good things so that your youth is renewed like the eagle's."* - **Psalm 103:1-5**

This passage reminds us to praise God for how good He has been. When we do this, we are refreshed and renewed. Whether we triumph or feel defeated, we should recall who and what God is. Doing so is greatly beneficial!

Say, for example, that we enter a time of prayer and God reveals His desire for us to seek new employment. The Bible says, *"But remember the Lord your God, for it is* **He who gives** *you the ability to produce wealth, and so confirms His covenant, which He swore to your forefathers, as it is today."* - **Deuteronomy 8:18** the correct response from us then would be to end our time of prayer with confidence that God will provide us a new job. We walk away with the conviction that God spoke, so it will come to pass!

Next we begin looking for openings and submitting resumes, remembering we must *execute* or (put action to) what we said or heard in prayer. Some time later a company we contacted, calls us to schedule an interview. Before and after the interview, we have complete faith based on our prayers, that the job is ours; so as expected, they offer us the position. It is at this time, we are taking the step of *experience* and we see the results of our execution. We prayed with understanding, and we heard from God. We took the time to get in front of God and come clean. We discovered scripture that resulted in our ability to get the revelation and confidence needed to execute new and powerful developments in our life. We ended our time of structured prayer in a prayerful state, and look what God did! Now, we're experiencing the manifestation of our prayers. How exciting!

Before we continue, please take note. The illustration used here was that of a *best case* scenario. All matters won't be resolved so quick and smooth. There will be times when our faith is tested for longer periods and the revelation we receive in prayer often takes longer than we expect to manifest. Yet, we must continue to build ourselves up in God and fight the good fight until all wars are won and all promises are possessed!

We will also need to spend time reflecting. We did everything correctly. We prayed, expected, executed, and now we have experienced God moving in our lives! What now? We must take time to acknowledge that this indeed was an act of *God*. Giving Him the credit and praise creates an atmosphere of appreciation and humility. It is in this atmosphere where our confidence is taken to a new and exciting level in God and prayer. It's when we reflect on the process and recall how it worked, that we grow to believe it's effectiveness for our lives and the lives of others! THIS is confidence; – knowing what we know to such an extent, know one can tell us different! So live in the moment, celebrate a while and think about the promises we found in the Bible before

113

our desires manifested. Doing this will fortifies our faith and prepares us to experience greater demonstrations of God's power in our lives!

When God moves in my life after I've prayed about something, I like to tell others about the experience as soon as possible in hopes of inspiring them. Maybe we didn't deserve that new job. Maybe we didn't try as hard as we should have at our last workplace. This causes us to recognize even more that *only* God could have made this happen for us. The Bible says, *"But **God** **chose** the foolish things of the world to shame the wise; **God** **chose** the weak things of the world to shame the strong."* **-1 Corinthians 1:27**. Looking back, we didn't deserve it, but God in His grace, blessed us. The point is that we remember that all good things come from the Lord and that He should be praised and receive our confidence!

I remember when I was hired for my current job, a job that provides well for my family, a job that pays more than any job I've ever had before! I lacked the experience and educational background my employer sought, but the one thing I did have was God. My pastor, the great Kerwin Manning, taught me that "God honors faithfulness". I remember this at all times. If I'm faithful to God, listen to Him and follow through on His Word, I can expect to win!

Brothers, although we've come a long way in our development, don't forsake this step! It is in this step that we are refreshed and recharged to press for more. The Bible says, *"They will tell of the power of your awesome works, and I will proclaim your great deeds. They will celebrate your **abundant goodness** and joyfully sing of your righteousness."* **-Psalm 145:6-7** God wants us to experience an abundance of His goodness. God consistently offers his blessings, but men are not always able to handle them. Begin telling Him, "Here I am Lord, bless me, I can handle it!"

How I take this step

"At this point in prayer I focus on recalling the many ways God has worked in my life on various occasions. By remembering all that He has done in my life and that I have done nothing outside of His grace.

I experience His love every time I do this because I'm reminded that God chose to bless me despite my unworthiness. Whenever God does this, which is often, I share my experiences with others. Perhaps my experiences will inspire them to allow God to work in their lives as well – this is my deepest desire!"

*E*XPERIENCE

PERSONAL THOUGHTS AND REFLECTIONS

_____

_____

_____

_____

_____

_____

_____

_____

_____

_____

_____

_____

_____

_____

_____

_____

_____

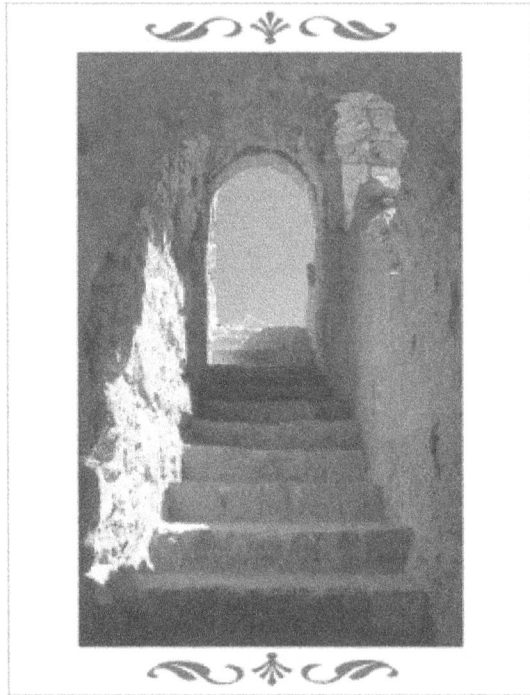

We are now ready to take the next step,
toward the place called Confidence!

Step XII
*E*mpower

The next and final step to reaching the place we call confidence is to empower. This means "to give power to, to sanction and endorse." One of my close friends and mentors Rusty Proctor taught me this: *"You can teach what you know, but you can only reproduce what you are."* So it's important to understand that as we *become* confident men of prayer, we are afforded the privilege and responsibility to now both, reproduce and endorse other confident men of prayer.

At this point, I'd like us to recall where *we* were before we picked up this book. We should consider the lack of understanding and structure we possessed and allow this to motivate us to lead other men in the way of becoming confident in prayer. Now, let's review some of what we discovered in reaching this step!

Prayer gives us access to God. Prayer gives us confidence to walk in faith. Prayer gives us the environment to receive revelation. Prayer gives us a "lifeline" when we don't know the answer. Prayer just keeps on giving and giving and giving! In view of this, why would we not want to share the steps we took to become confident in prayer with our brothers? How can we walk around with confidence and watch our brother struggle, especially when, before long, they will notice our newly attained confidence – it's like the sweet aroma coming from a neighborhood bakery at 5am, it can't be ignored!

Think about the last time you smelled your favorite pastries baking in the oven as you walked into a bakery for a cup of coffee. Remember how good it smelled and how captivated you were. Remember how you couldn't wait to get closer to the source of the smell. You just had to have a taste for yourself.

The same is true in regards to confidence! When we walk around with confidence, others take note. They "smell" it on us, and it is our duty to envelop them in the same aroma. How dare we walk around smelling of power, hope and assurance while allowing our brother to remain unsure?

I think it's important to state; men are attracted to confidence, not arrogance! Charisma and style can be manipulated to appear as confidence, but the test is in our hearts. How do I know if I'm genuinely confident or have fallen into arrogance? Humility! Humility says - our confidence is in God's ability, not in our own. When we notice others drawing attention to their abilities and strengths, chances are a "fall" is approaching. The Bible says, *"Pride goes before destruction, a haughty spirit **before a fall.**"* **-Proverbs 16:18**. In fact, God despises this kind of behavior. *"To fear the Lord is to **hate evil**; I hate pride and arrogance, evil behavior and perverse speech."* **-Proverbs 8:13**, this is why the experience step is so important, it keeps things in proper perspective!

I encourage you to begin using these steps in prayer and to acknowledge that you have the ability to reproduce other confident men of prayer. I authorize you to begin telling other men about the joy and confidence that you now possess. I urge you to share this book with other men and begin walking with them through these steps.

We are all created to have impact and influence, to reproduce after our own kind, not only in the physical sense, but the spiritual as well. We should be about the business of producing spiritual sons born from the confidence we now have. The Bible says that a tree is known by its fruit—fruit symbolizing that which comes from inside of you.

Men of prayer, take notice of who's around you and begin with them. They may be men in your church or an accountability group. Whoever they are, tell them that you have found peace, order and most of all *CONFIDENCE* in your prayer life and that they can find it too!

My continual prayer is that we will cultivate the courage and confidence through prayer to go outside of ourselves and help other men. No matter our careers, locations, backgrounds or ethnic groups, our ultimate purpose is to give. Brothers, until we learn to give away what we have, we'll never have room to receive what God wants to give to us!

So, let's begin today and empower our brothers, by leading them through the *Corridor to Confidence*.

How I take this step

"I seek to identify the men in my sphere who are trying to live righteously and invite them to a time of prayer. I make time in my week to sit with these men and offer them what I know. I also sit with men who serve as mentors to me.

This allows me to experience continued growth. I don't wait until my life or schedule is perfect to begin this process because I figure they never will be. So, like Nike - "I just do it!"

*E*MPOWER

PERSONAL THOUGHTS AND REFLECTIONS

_____

_____

_____

_____

_____

_____

_____

_____

_____

_____

_____

_____

_____

_____

_____

_____

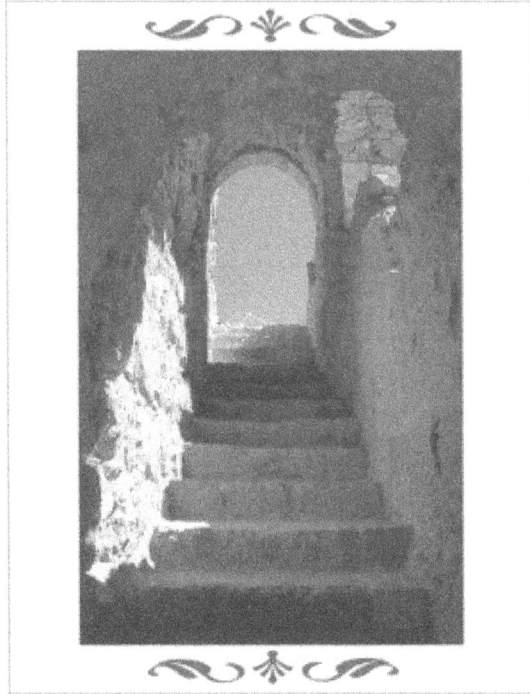

Congratulations,
We have now reached the place called Confidence!

Continuing through the Corridor

Whether you are a beginner or have been praying for years, it is my hope that this journey has helped you cultivate greater levels of confidence in your prayer life! As we began, your level of expectation may have not been great, but I believe you now have good reason to expect more from yourself, life and God. Now, let's revisit the steps that led to this moment!

We began this journey with an *explanation*; we discovered what prayer is and why we need it. We then learned to identify our *expectations* of God and prayer. From there, we created room for God's presence and power to operate by *eliminating* our distractions. We learned that in order to develop confidence we need to be thankful and grateful, reminding ourselves and God of how much we *esteem* Him. Next we gave God His due respect by *exalting* Him aloud and with conviction. This moved us to a place of trust and openness that allowed us to *expose* the sin in our lives. With our newfound freedom, we were able to handle the Word of God and *extract* its wisdom! With His Word we were able to *establish* the confidence to demand of life new results; knowing God hears us! After this, we allowed God to *edify* us in the Truth of His Word, not the lies of this world. We then made our *exit*, continuing in our fellowship while remaining attentive for opportunities to *execute* His Word. This positioned us to *experience* the power of prayer for ourselves and giving us the conviction to *empower* others by sharing our results and what we learned!

Brothers, we've taken all the steps necessary to enter into the place called confidence and make it our home! We are no longer missing the structure we need for prayer. Now, all we have to do is remain determined to stay on course. This takes endurance, so learn to pace yourself; begin slowly and master each step. You have the rest of your life to pray. Don't overwhelm yourself with it all in one day. Allow room for error and include others in your journey. God is not looking for Super-*man*. He's looking for prayerful *men*!

Warning:

*Those who choose to enter
this corridor
must do so with care,
for the revelation and
confidence obtained
are powerful and effective,
and have been proven
to get results!*

Let us pray!

The Corridor to Confidence
Visual Target Graph

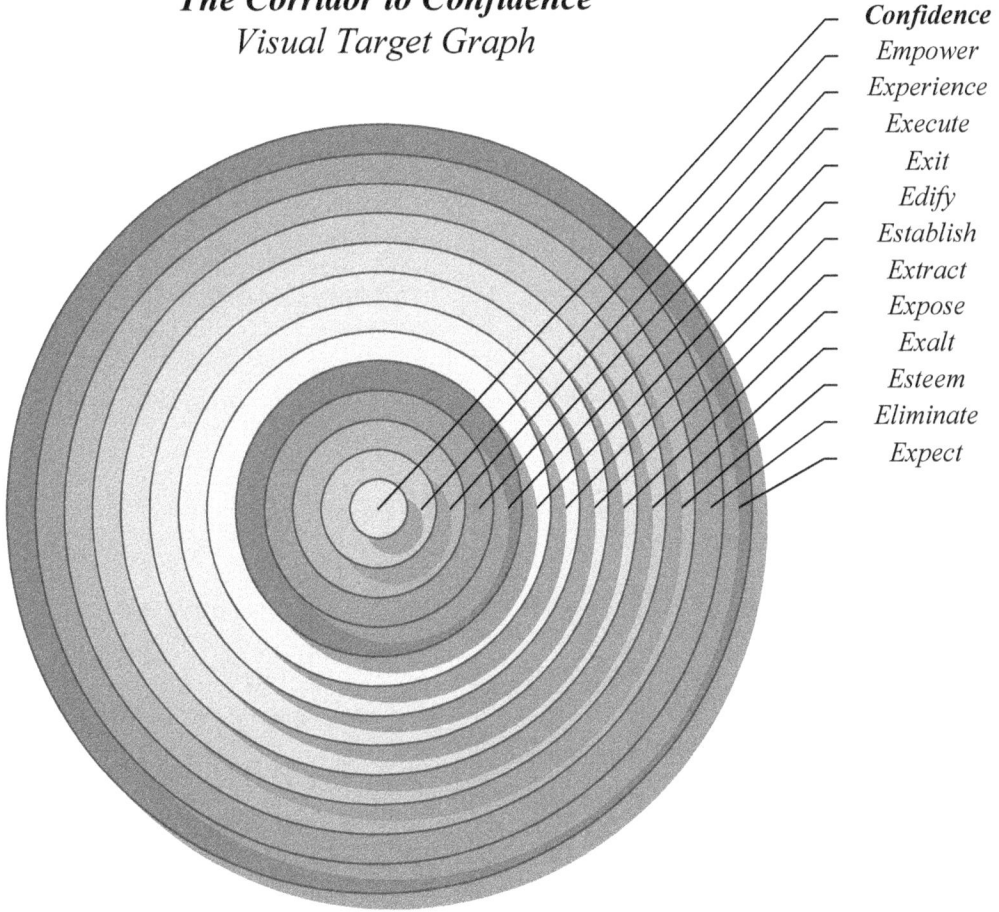

Confidence
Empower
Experience
Execute
Exit
Edify
Establish
Extract
Expose
Exalt
Esteem
Eliminate
Expect

Use this graph to remind yourself of the "Bull's-eye" like focus you are cultivating in prayer. By following these steps; you will always hit your target!

Master Prayer Plan
"Quick Reference Guide"
Use this as a handy reminder for when you're "on the go"

Expect- To be _Inspired_. You must believe that you will leave prayer as an improved man!

Eliminate- The _Distractions_ of life. Make private time with God a priority!

Esteem- _God_ for His grace and mercy. Thank Him for His goodness!

Exalt- The _Name_ of the Lord. Place His name above your own and the challenges of life!

Expose- The _Sin_ in your life. Come clean, and be completely honest!

Extract- _Knowledge_ from the Word of God. Seek understanding. Expect revelation!

Establish- A time of _Communion_ with God. Make requests based on His Word and intercede for others!

Edify- _Yourself_ in the Truth of God's Word!

Exit- _Confidently_. Know that you prayed correctly and that God heard you_!_

Execute-The _Word_ you've discovered and any instructions given by God!

Experience- The _Power_ of God through results and reflection.

Empower- _Others_ to do what you now know how to do, pray with confidence!

About the Author

Pastor Treveal C.W. Lynch is the Co-founder and C.E.O of Treveal Lynch Ministries International (**T.L.M.I.**), a ministry in the business of shepherding man's confidence back to God and His Kingdom. Often referred to as *"The voice they listen to"*, Treveal is an anointed teacher, speaker, writer and entrepreneur who has effectively communicated the Word of God for over 8 years. Through a forthright, no-nonsense approach, his presentation of the gospel both convicts and encourages those in attendance.

Under the extraordinary leadership of his spiritual parents and exemplars Pastors Kerwin and Madelyn Manning (Pasadena Church), and a host of spiritual and professional leaders from around the country, Treveal has learned to serve God through an unlimited ministry model and developed a strict adherence to the principles of God.

Enthused by his vision to see people, *specifically* men pray successfully, Treveal continues to lead weekly prayer gatherings and offer one on one coaching for prayer development to groups and individuals. Future plans include the development and implementation of an international prayer curriculum to be taught in churches and homes worldwide.

Treveal is quoted as saying *"I believe we are rapidly approaching a time in our society when God's way will no longer be the best way, but the only way to succeed! It is our responsibility to effectively communicate the truth of this message for future generations."*

Treveal and his wife Andrea have been married and ministering together for over 8 blissful years. They have four beautiful children – Treveal Jr., Angelyce, Aaron and Tyler. They currently reside in Pasadena, Ca.

"Contrary to popular belief and practice, the purpose of prayer is not to solicit God for the things we believe we need.
But rather, to invite God's influence in repossessing what already belongs to us."

- Treveal C.W. Lynch

For more information contact us at:

Treveal Lynch Ministries International
P.O. Box 12
Pasadena, Ca 91102-0012

Or visit us online at:

www.tlmionline.com

Copyright © 2008 Treveal Lynch Ministries International

www.ingramcontent.com/pod-product-compliance
Lightning Source LLC
Chambersburg PA
CBHW032005040426
42448CB00006B/493

* 9 7 8 0 6 1 5 2 1 7 3 5 2 *